*Dear
Music Lover...*

By the same author

MY MUSIC

MUSICIAN AT LARGE: an autobiography

TO CHINA WITH LOVE: the story of Joseph & Hannah Race

Dear Music Lover...

Steve Race

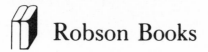 Robson Books

for P. F.

FIRST PUBLISHED IN GREAT BRITAIN IN 1981 BY
ROBSON BOOKS LTD., 28 POLAND STREET,
LONDON W1V 3DB. COPYRIGHT © 1981 STEVE
RACE

Printed by Spottiswoode Ballantyne Ltd, Colchester and London

CONTENTS

1

Dear Music Lover

Thank you for your letter, which has been forwarded to me by the BBC. How I agree with you on the subject of Tchaikovsky's *1812 Overture*! It's a monster.

More to the point, perhaps, Tchaikovsky seems to have agreed with you, too. In a letter written to a lady friend while he was busy composing that pompous score, Tchaikovsky described the work to her as 'very noisy', adding (with astounding honesty) that it seemed to him to have 'no great artistic value'. Strong words, when you consider the desperate love affair that normally exists between a creative artist and his current brainchild! The composer ended his letter by saying that he was writing the overture 'without much enthusiasm'. I imagine he might have been less than pleased at its continuing success a century later at the expense of his more worthwhile creations. But then one or two things have happened to Tchaikovsky's music over recent years that might not have delighted him.

Do you know about the première of *1812*? It was due to take place at the Cathedral of Our Saviour in Moscow, where an enormous orchestra, augmented with batteries of percussion instruments, was to play outside the great doors. Batteries of another kind were to be wired to electric circuits, and these—

operated by switches beside the conductor's rostrum—would trigger off gunfire at key dramatic moments. As a final touch of the Barnum and Baileys, all the church bells in Moscow would chime in unison (or at any rate, simultaneously). Altogether it was an ambitious scheme, not unlike the setting for one of today's disaster movies—indeed ripe for catastrophe.

In the event the grandiose plan did not materialize. Tchaikovsky's *Festival Overture, 1812*—that's the proper title— was given its somewhat tame first performance two years later in 1882 at an exhibition, without any of the cannon, bombs, mortars or fireworks with which today's audiences are alternately shattered and delighted. As for Tchaikovsky himself, he lived for another 13 years and redeemed his good name with a number of far less tiresome works, which varied from the E minor Symphony to *The Nutcracker*.

The friend to whom he wrote that frank letter about the progress of the overture was Madame Von Meck, a lady of distinction, wealth and rare understanding, who supported the unhappy man through some of his most difficult years, but without—and surely this is remarkable for a woman— insisting on meeting him in order that he could fall in love with her person as well as with her soul.

In fact they never did meet in the flesh. This odd but fortunate association led a music student to write in an exam paper that '. . . Tchaikovsky never married, but an old lady gave him an annual alliance'. Poor man, even a once-a-year alliance was denied him, both by luck and by inclination. Still, we must be glad that he was spared the ultimate misery of seeing Ken Russell's film version of his life.

My best advice to you regarding the clamorous, padded, overblown and over-performed *1812 Overture* is to avoid it wherever possible. After all, there are many other good years in music, aren't there? 1685 and 1786, for instance. Not to mention 1921.

Yours sincerely

2

2

Yes, I suppose my reference to 1685, 1786 and 1921 as vintage musical years must have been somewhat obscure. Before going on to explain, may I say how glad I am that you have come clean and given me your name, rather than continuing to hide under a *nom de plume*, however apt?

The fault may be mine, but *noms de plume* (I assume that is the correct plural) tend to make me suspect a touch of cowardice on the part of a correspondent; or something I dislike even more, namely archness. Calling yourself 'Music lover' at the start of your first letter was technically correct, of course. You, my dear sir, are an *amateur* of music in the old, delightful expression meaning one who loves the art. But now you have an actual name so much the better. May I call you Pat?— Thank you.

I wrote of 1685 as being 'a good year'. No doubt you looked it up, and found that it was the year of the revocation of the Edict of Nantes, an event (whatever it may be) that a certain up-market daily paper reminds us of once a year under *The Day's Anniversaries*. But the good thing about 1685 was that it saw the births of both Bach (J. S.) and Handel (G. F.). That makes it an important date by any artistic standards.

Did you know that one of the most important men in the

3

annals of music knew both Bach and Handel and played an important role in their lives, though the two composers themselves never met? The person who had dealings with both of them was an itinerant medical man. I don't know his name, but he treated both composers for eye trouble, and succeeded in virtually blinding both of them.

What an achievement for one simple medico! I sometimes wonder whether Bach and Handel, now the best of friends no doubt and with their sight restored in the Elysian Fields, have considered going off together in search of that quack and settling their account with him at long last. If they did, I suspect it would have been Bach who took a heavy cudgel, and Handel who said, 'Don't hit him too hard, Johann.'

In the list of great musical years in my previous letter I mentioned 1921 merely because it was the year of my own birth. Miniscule jokes like that have a way of rebounding on one, but I hope you didn't waste too much time puzzling over whom I can have meant! Far more worthy of your researches was 1786, my favourite year of the three, simply because of what Mozart managed to do in those twelve short months.

He was 30 years old, the age at which many of us are just beginning to think about settling down to some proper work at last. Behind him were almost 500 individual compositions varying from operas and symphonies to serenades and songs. He was a busy, prolific young musician, with enough master-pieces already completed to represent for anyone else a long life's work, as well as to assure them of immortality.

But here he was at 30, and his immediate task was to write some piano concertos to play at his own public concert appearances.

So on 2 March 1786 he completed the A major piano Concerto (listed now as K. 488) and another in C minor (K. 491) a mere 22 days later. Not a bad month's work on the whole.

The A major Concerto in particular is a marvel, from its businesslike opening tune drenched in that special Mozart sunshine—

—through a heart-stopping slow movement—

—to the tight, purposeful finale.

But having completed K. 488 and 491, indisputably two of the greatest piano concertos in all music, Mozart did not sit back and claim a sabbatical for the rest of 1786. He wrote the fourth horn concerto: the one that ends with that stuttering tune which Flanders and Swann turned into a song about learning to play the horn—

Also from that same amazing year came yet another piano concerto, then a masterpiece of a piano quartet in E flat, the joyfully swinging D major Quartet (K. 499), a dozen or more lesser, works, and the *Prague Symphony*. Then, no doubt in order to stave off any accusations of laziness, he rounded off the twelvemonth with the première of *The Marriage of Figaro*, adding *Don Giovanni* the following year!

No wonder most serious musicians regard Mozart as a composer completely in a class by himself. There is a story told of the conductor, Bruno Walter, who was asked which composer could be said to have given him the most pleasure and satisfaction.

'Beethoven,' he replied. Then he paused, and added, 'Wagner . . . Mahler . . . Bruckner . . . Oh, there are so many!'

'But surely, maestro, what about Mozart?'

'Oh,' said Bruno Walter, 'naturally I assumed you meant among the *others*.'

It was not Bruno Walter, though it might well have been, who coined the pleasant fancy about life in heaven: that when the angels sing for God's benefit they sing Beethoven's music. But when they sing for themselves, they sing Mozart—and God eavesdrops.

I do hope you will remind me to get enthusiastic about Mozart in some future letter—assuming there *are* any future letters, of course. That's up to you. If there's no reply, I can take a hint.

Yours sincerely

Steve (Race)

3

Dear Pat Ford

Miss Pat Ford! My mistake! I see it all now. In my male chauvinist pig-like way I had assumed that the name *Pat* was short for Patrick. Now I learn that it is short for Patricia I realize why you were not entirely charmed with my reference to Madame Von Meck. What was it I wrote in that first letter?—'She supported him through some of his most difficult years, but without—and surely this is remarkable for a woman—insisting on meeting him in order that he could fall in love with her person as well as with her soul.'

I take it back. That remark could have cost me your subsequent letters, which would have been a pity because now I find that you, like me, are a Mozart case. It forges a bond between us: a similar bond to the one which united poor old Tchaikovsky and *his* pen-pal, the proud and altogether praiseworthy Madame Von Meck. (How's that for making restitution?)

No, I didn't catch the offending broadcast, as it happens, but I know the work well and your anger on hearing the pop version of Mozart's Fortieth Symphony in G minor does you credit. I shall keep your letter in a special file as an example of how to condemn someone to eternal hellfire while yet remaining ladylike and holding on grimly to one's syntax. What the pop industry has done to that enchanting symphony (and to others, like Beethoven's seventh) is indeed criminal.

And ought to be banned? Aha, of that I am not so sure.

I think it is important to be clear in one's mind as to *why* it is reprehensible to make beat versions of baroque classics; what exactly constitute the rather special circumstances under which adaptations, arrangements, transcriptions and modernizations might perhaps be condoned. I certainly do not go along with those who airily condemn every example of what they call 'jazzing the classics'. Theirs is not really a tenable position. Let's examine it.

Mozart was not a saint. (Very far from it, as you will know if you have read his letters or seen Peter Schaffer's play, *Amadeus*.) A genius, he was; a saint, he was not. So most of his music takes its place alongside the other *secular* joys which mankind has produced down the ages. My point is that, with the obvious exception of the *Requiem* and a few other works, Mozart's music is not part of anyone's deepest religious experience. I would oppose the right of any musician to demean for popular consumption the *B minor Mass* of Bach, Elgar's *Dream of Gerontius* or Max Bruch's *Kol Nidrei*. So, I hope, would any decent person, on the grounds that sincere people could be genuinely hurt by such an act. There are enough opportunities for musical arrangers and popularizers to exercise their talents without tampering with the handful of truly sacrosanct works.

Agreed? Right. But even by this stage of the argument the case is somewhat complicated, due to the awkward fact that Mozart himself cheerfully tampered with Handel's *Messiah*. He re-scored it, making fairly considerable changes to that master-piece which Handelians believe to have been directly inspired from above, and hence hardly capable of 'improvement', even by young Mozart.

'Ah,' you may say, 'but that's a case of one genius bending his mind to the work of another genius. By that yardstick, Mozart's views on Handel are of legitimate artistic interest, whereas James Last's view on Beethoven, or Tomita's moog-synthesizings on Debussy, are not.'

True perhaps. Yet where are we to draw the line? Line-drawing is never easy and here it is almost impossible. When Jacques Loussier performs a Bach fugue more or less as the composer would have wished it to be played but then a moment later drags it screaming into swing-time, is he committing an artistic crime? Or is he merely expressing a fine but tiny item of eighteenth-century secular music in terms of late-twentieth-century taste?

The nagging thought begins to arise: would Carnegie Hall in New York, the Royal Albert Hall in London or wherever Loussier may appear, be as full of happy listeners for a straightforward Bach fugue recital as they are for Loussier, the Swingles or Wendy Carlos? Looking back over the past century, did not Tin Pan Alley do as much ultimately for Tchaikovsky as the concert promoters of his own day?

I ask the question; let me go on to answer it in my own way. If demeaning the great classics is the only means of bringing them into favour with the masses then I think I would rather that the masses went without them. After all, not much further down that road lie some baleful bowdlerisms: *Fragrant Moments with Tristan and Isolde, Singalong with Monteverdi, Kyrie Reggae* . . . and in the literary line I suppose we might have *Favourite Battles from War and Peace*.

Speaking for myself, I have never subscribed to the view that reducing the intellectual demands of great art does any more than tend to cheapen the product, though I am aware that there are people who firmly believe the opposite. They claim to know of youngsters who have arrived at a state of Wagnerian bliss through happening to catch a radio performance of the *Parsifal Cha-cha* or *Prize Song Boogie*. I can only say that it hasn't happened to anyone I know.

And yet . . . and yet. How can we possibly counsel a flat ban on the re-thinking, re-scoring or re-arranging of established works? That would be to rule out at a stroke Liszt's transcriptions from Wagner and Verdi, Britten's Purcell-based *Young Person's Guide to the Orchestra*, Beethoven's *Diabelli Variations*, even the harmless enough adaptations that became *Lilac Time, Song of Norway* and *Kismet*. All those pleasures would be denied us if we told the world's re-arrangers to keep their filthy hands off existing works. And the loss would be inconceivable. No more *Air on the G String*?

A particularly tricky example in this connection is the famous opening C major Prelude from J. S. Bach's *48 Preludes and Fugues*. Poor old Bach no doubt thought it perfectly adequate in the form in which he left the prelude: an ingenious and pleasing sequence of related arpeggios.

But then along came Gounod, another respected composer of impeccable musical background and roughly comparable pedigree, who took one look at Bach's little piece and decided to improve on it. Treating the chord structure as if it were merely an accompaniment, he added a completely new and extraneous (not to say highly emotional) melody over the top, calling the finished article his—or rather Bach/Gounod's— *Ave Maria*.

Bach would scarcely have approved, claiming no doubt that if he had thought the piece needed a 'tune' he would have given it one. Yet, if Gounod had held off on the grounds of taste or artistic integrity, the repertoire of religious melody would have been very much the poorer. I submit that it is an untenable position for us to take up: Bach sacred, Gounod sacred; Bach/ Gounod *verboten*.

Remember that Bach himself was an eager arranger of other people's works. He re-scored Vivaldi violin concertos for harpsichord or organ, taking liberties with them which no modern scholar would condone. *Wachet Auf*, one of J. S. Bach's best loved 'compositions', seems to have been derived from a piece by Philip Nicolai dated 1599, the best part of a century before Bach was born. Dr. Albert Schweitzer, Bach-addicted though he was, admitted that Bach even abused his *own* works at times, notably the C minor Concerto for two violins which he transcribed none too faithfully for harpsichord. How he could bring himself so to desecrate the slow movement was beyond Schweitzer's understanding. 'Had he not done it himself, we should be protesting in his name today against so un-Bachlike a transcription,' wrote the good doctor, adding that such activities made it 'hard for his prophets to go forth

10

in the name of Bach against the evil transcribers'.

So the problem is far from being an easy one, however much one may be tempted to 'go forth'. Perhaps all we can say for sure is this: if Musician B tampers with the work of Musician A he does so at his artistic peril. If Musician B is an honest craftsman with some talent and a proper respect for the original, like the man who adapted Schubert's tunes for *Lilac Time*, then the result will probably be acceptable to most music lovers, and rather more than acceptable to many.

If Musician B happens to be Ralph Vaughan Williams, he can turn the simple 450-year-old *Greensleeves* into something new and lovely without in the least destroying the original. That original still remains, whole, available and enjoyable, for those who prefer its purer form. In the same way Dvorak's *Humoresque* remains as a fiddle favourite for those who (unlike me, as it happens) prefer its salon gentility to the brisk Art Tatum transcription for jazz piano; brilliant, involved, but far indeed from the composer's initial concept. As that thoughtful music man, Sidney Harrison, has pointed out, re-arranging a classic is like subjecting a cathedral to *Son et Lumière*. Once you turn the light off, the original is still there, whole and un-harmed.

This much surely we have to concede. Otherwise a flat and absolute ban on the activities of *any* Musician B at all would rob us of much magnificent music, including the Brahms *Academic Festival Overture*, which is based on pop hits of 1880. (Yes, it works that way round as well!) If the art of the arranger is to be prohibited, the adoring James Galway public would be robbed of all those adaptations for flute which the ebullient Galway has fashioned out of music never intended for his instrument in the first place. A loss indeed—ask anybody. Ask Jimmy.

As for Mussorgsky . . . Well, I really don't know where we would stand on *that* subject. His fellow composers found it almost impossible to keep their improving hands off Mussorgsky's scores, in fact a good part of the past century has been devoted to restoring the composer's original ideas after the meddling to which his friends had subjected them.

11

Mussorgsky is best known nowadays for his *Pictures at an Exhibition* which he conceived for piano solo. But a succession of later musicians, notably Ravel, felt that the music would be more effective if scored for full symphony orchestra; and it has to be said that in this they were correct. It *is* more effective as an orchestral experience, especially since Mussorgsky's original manuscript was not notably pianistic.

Recently, to complicate matters further, Elgar Howarth has scored the work brilliantly for brass choir. Isao Tomita has fashioned the whole suite into a scintillating long-playing record for moog synthesizer. So in this long and complicated history of re-scoring, re-thinking and re-evaluation, who are the iniquitous Musicians B? And should every one of them have been refused access to Mussorgsky's original, on principle?

That popped-up Mozart Symphony in G minor, though. . . Ugh! You're right about that. Speaking for myself—and pleading that everyone should be permitted just one irrational act which is contrary to his own most liberal judgements—I would cheerfully burn all available copies of it in the market-place at Salzburg. The one sure way to kill the sheer joyousness of Mozart's music is to force it into a metronomic beat, pound it out *double-forte* and give it over to the disco dancers.

As for you, my dear Miss Ford, may heaven preserve your vitriolic pen, and deliver you at life's end to your personal cloud in a sunlit heaven, where the mains supply is 97½ volts and there are no screaming pop guitarists or amplified rock drummers. . . Not even an electric harp. Just Mozart, waiting with a smile of welcome on his face, to offer you K. 626. I wonder what it is?

Yours sincerely

Steve (Race)

12

4

Dear Pat

—As you are kind enough to suggest that I should call you. And why not? We seem to have a lot in common, musically speaking. Despite what I suspect is a grotesque difference in our ages, I hope you will call me Steve. That, anyway, is how I shall sign myself.

So you are a singer. Good! No doubt you know John Wesley's wise words about singing, written for the preface to his hymnbook: 'Sing lustily and with good courage. Beware of singing as if you were half dead or asleep.' Good sound advice. But then almost immediately afterwards he writes: 'Sing *modestly*. Do not bawl, so that you may not destroy the harmony. Sing in time. Do not run, nor stay behind the time. Take care not to sing too slow. This drawling way naturally steals upon all who are lazy and it is high time to drive it out from among us and sing all our tunes as quick as we did at first.'

Wesley's followers certainly had plenty of precepts to carry in mind as they chanted the Wesley hymns. But their leader was right: singing can easily become sloppy and self-indulgent.

Another favourite quotation of mine on the subject comes from the great Elizabethan composer, William Byrd: 'Since singing is so good a thing I wish all men would learn to sing.'

Notice the implied emphasis, Pat, on the word *learn*; not just 'everyone should sing' but 'everyone should *learn* to sing'. Singing is one of those activities like swimming, driving a car or making love that are most effectively done under a certain amount of skilled guidance. No doubt one can flounder ashore somehow, find the brake by a process of elimination or do one's own thing in a haystack. But the best results come with a few properly organized lessons.

That, at any rate, is the customary received wisdom. Is music perhaps different in that respect, though, especially nowadays? Is it *necessary* to be taught?

Over the years I have known a good many gifted musical people who on the whole might not have benefited all that much from formal tuition. Paul McCartney took lessons for a while from a friend of mine who is a 'serious' composer. He was determined to master the notation of music and learn something of its theory. But in the end he gave up, deciding perhaps that his natural ear and gift for invention might come to be affected by technical considerations. So he abandoned the lessons and continued to make his music in a purely instinctive way, employing (as he could well afford to do) someone else to take down the tunes and organize the notation of the harmonies whenever he felt the creative juices begin to rise.

I suspect McCartney may have had a point. It is certainly true that some of the best Beatles songs break the elementary rules that any wideawake teacher would have insisted upon being observed.

A case in point is *Michelle*. The chord which supports the second bar is actually 'wrong' for the melody note—

If I, or someone like me, had been present at the recording session with a pencil and five seconds to spare, we would have been tempted to 'correct' either the chord or the tune.

'Allow me, Paul,' we would have said politely—with resulting damage to a fine and original song. I suppose after one or two more lessons from my composer friend Paul McCartney might have spotted the 'error' for himself, and *Michelle* would not have been quite *Michelle*. A sad loss to music.

Norwegian Wood, another striking Beatles tune, might easily have taken a different form if its composer had studied the standard song repertoire rather than merely done his own melodic thing.

'I once had a girl, or should I say she once had me?' runs the opening line. A good many musicians trained in the logical virtues of melodic sequence would have stated the *first four* notes just as the Beatles did, but then repeated them precisely, on different degrees of the scale, making a shapely and symmetrical triple phrase—

Not so the Beatles. In their hands the first line of *Norwegian Wood* uses three quite distinct melodic shapes, owing nothing to sequence, in fact deliberately avoiding it. At the word 'once' the melody leaps up to a splendidly unexpected note, as effective in its way as the melodic jump at the final rhetorical question 'where *do* they all come from?' in that superb song, *Eleanor Rigby*.

To teach then, or not to teach? To learn music or deliberately not to do so?

I wonder sometimes what Bob Dylan would have sounded like if a really determined singing teacher could have got him to sign on for some quick voice production lessons before the recording company found him. That nasal tone: clearly it issues from the 'wrong' place, doesn't it? While his tendency to smear the notes from one to another in that reprehensible way of his could be eradicated by a strict course in scales and vocal exercises. And, my dear, that tortured diction! Get the lad singing o-pen vow-els, that'll cure him. The result of such

15

discipline would have been marked: a non-career for Robert Zimmerman, instead of world fame for Bob Dylan, far less general happiness around the place and a lot of hungry promoters and agents littering the streets.

An example nearer to my own generation, and perhaps nearer to my heart by an inch or two, is that of Louis Armstrong. By all the rules Louis should never have been allowed to sing at all, but told sternly to stick to his trumpet playing and leave singing to those with a voice.

In the strictest sense he *couldn't* sing, could he? All he could do was express his own happy-go-lucky personality through a kind of glottal croak. And, of course, that was the very secret on which his vocal success was founded: nothing could have delighted the listeners more.

It remains as true in the 1980s as it was in the 1920s that if you wish to entertain your fellow men (yes, and *women*, Pat) you should either blind them with artistry or perform exactly like they do after a couple of drinks. You must be either one of the gods or one of the lads. That's where popular success lies—at both ends of the virtuoso ladder. It's the ones in the middle of the ladder who need strong finger-nails.

As for Louis Armstrong, his appeal was precisely to those of us whose voices are croaky like his. Not that he was easy to categorize according to the established pigeonholes of popular music.

'Are you a folk singer?' some earnest enquirer once asked.

Louis thought hard. 'Folk singer? Guess I must be,' he replied. 'I ain't never heard a horse sing.'

Armstrong's idiosyncratic voice delighted the world for half a century, because in popular music and jazz the performer's personality is more important than the composer's score—always. To put it another way, the medium beats the message nowadays.

Middle-aged and elderly music lovers who rail at today's pop sounds make a big mistake on this very point. They forget that a pop record in the 1980s is intended to be a complete, unified experience: song, singers, instrumentalists and recording engineers pooling their contributions in order to make a combined, indivisible sound that will tease the public's ear for a week or two.

That's all. To anguish over the inadequacies of a transient pop single is as pointless as preserving last night's evening paper and expecting it to make good reading tomorrow. Yesterday's paper is a dead thing to anyone except a historian, and so is yesterday's top-of-the-pops, created as it was to give instant entertainment for a flash of time. No one expects more, no one wants more.

A pop record, then, offers a moment's pleasure through a quick self-contained emotional experience. Fatuous to complain, as some people still do, that they 'can't hear the words' on a pop disc. What words? Who wants to hear them? They are probably not worth hearing anyway, being intended merely as a vehicle for a snatch of melody or for a mood; a moment's impact. 'Rifol rifol tolle-riddle i-doh,' chanted the eighteenth-century countryman at the village inn, waving his pint of scrumpy. 'Tolle *what?*' demanded his grandfather. 'Can't hear you. Sing up, lad. Let's hear the words!'

As for the much vaunted superiority of popular song lyrics in the old days, I'm not so sure that the old days (some of which I remember) were quite as fruitful as we like to think. No doubt we *could* clearly hear the words in the Twenties and Thirties when Belle Mooney crooned, 'We wandered, me and you, beneath the lovers' moon; but childhood in the wildwood was ended all too soon . . .' It might have been better if we had not been able to hear nine-tenths of those mediocre old songs. There wasn't a *Smoke gets in your Eyes* every month in our teens, even if we now like to think there was.

Another point. What we cared about in those days was the song itself. Going into a record shop we would ask the assistant, 'Have you got a record of *Love me True?*'

'Let's see,' the assistant would reply. (Assistants assisted the customer in those days.) 'Let's see, we've got recordings of it by Bing Crosby, Sharkey's Jazz Hounds, a military band, a cinema organ, Paul Robeson and Spike Jones. Which one would you like?'

17

After playing a chorus or so of each one—those *were* the days, my friend!—we would make our choice and leave the shop with, under our arm, what amounted to simply a *song*, performed by someone or other on a wax disc.

That is the greatest change of all. No youngster goes into a record shop these days for 'a record of somebody doing *Hound Dog*'. He wants Elvis Presley or nothing. The song *is* the performance; the performance *is* the song.

All this, Pat, because you mentioned the fact that you sing. What sort of music do you sing, I wonder? Alone, or with others? Are you—I hope I have the expression right—'into punk'? And bearing in mind William Byrd's remark, have you learnt to sing? Or do you, in the immortal words of the old music hall comic, just 'open your mouth and push'?

I am convinced that there is a lot to be said for the untrained as well as the trained approach to vocalism, depending on what kind of music you choose to sing. Meanwhile I suppose we ought to amend William Byrd's remark in the light of more recent musical activities. 'Since singing is so good a thing, I wish all men would learn to sing ... Except for Louis Armstrong, Fats Waller, Bob Dylan, Gene Kelly, Elvis Presley, Noël Coward, Mick Jagger ...'

And Pat Ford? I wonder.

Yours

Steve

5

Dear Pat

So you're a member of a choir! To tell the truth I half suspected
it, indeed I hoped for it. Yours is a mixed choir, I trust: they're
much more fun than those single sex groups. I hope you have a
male conductor; a holy terror whom every female member of
the choir fears, resents and complains about endlessly.

There is something curiously masochistic about membership of an amateur choir. It is as if one wanted to express one's
individual artistic personality, yet at the same time to be
dominated; to be musically creative, yet one of the crowd. And
compounding the paradox, every choir is ultimately as good as
its individuals—providing they are ready to sink their
individuality! It's all very odd.

Stimulating too, of course. When you come to think about it,
singing is one of the relatively few activities that combine a
strong artistic satisfaction with an element of physical exercise.
(It beats authorship and flower arranging any day.) If your
choir is a good one you will feel both deeply uplifted and totally
exhausted at the end of a rehearsal.

The degree of achievement you feel after an hour or two's
choir practice is likely to be governed by a straightforward
consideration, namely what percentage of choir members can
read music at sight. Those who cannot read tend rather to drag

the others back. Having to have their notes played or sung over to them and dinned into their memories by rote is a painful process, for them as well as for you.

Not that reading music—I'm sure you know this already—is quite the same thing as sight-singing. I know a much admired pianist who can read a Chopin study at sight without pausing for breath, yet vocally speaking he couldn't pitch an interval of a diminished fifth. (As, by the way, I once heard a cuckoo do, so it can't be all that difficult.)

I hope you are a little in love with the conductor of your choir and he with you. Eyes glued to one another at brief but significant moments, you sing—and he mouths—the chorus words at your annual *Messiah*, *Elijah* or *Creation*. Do his eyes rest on you while the tenor soloist in Haydn's score tells of Adam and Eve's first encounter?

> *A man, the lord and king of nature all . . .*
> *With fondness leans upon his breast*
> *The partner for him form'd,*
> *A woman, fair and graceful spouse;*
> *Her softly smiling virgin looks . . .*
> *Bespeak him love and joy and bliss!*

Your conductor wouldn't be the first musical director of a mixed choir to take advantage of those lines to transfix some adoring lady member with A Special Look.

But I'm romancing: back to technicalities. Choral conductors always mouth the words, and this is useful for two reasons: it helps the singers to keep their place, and it reminds them to open their mouths (as they are forever being told to do). In this word-mouthing the choir conductor differs from his orchestral counterpart, who most emphatically must *not* sing, though some do. A few even grunt audibly.

It is tempting to suggest that while choral conductors exist for the choir's benefit, orchestral conductors exist for the benefit of the audience. Certainly a good many professional players would agree. It is an indisputable fact that for large stretches of the average symphony concert the orchestral conductor is simply not needed.

Once a good professional orchestra is launched into *Eine Kleine Nachtmusik* or a *Brandenburg Concerto* it has no real need for a conductor to be there, disporting himself on a raised platform, following the tempo with one arm and assisting the players to count eight bar rests with the other. Admittedly the initial tempo needs to be set. But the leader of the violins is quite capable of doing that with a simple lift of his shoulders and a purposeful down-stroke of his bow. After that the music more or less plays itself.

What then is the orchestral conductor for? When is he of use?

The answer is: when there is a change of tempo, a slowing down or speeding up to be negotiated; whenever there is a pause in the music and consequently a decision to be made over how long to hold a note or a silence; when the music being performed is of sufficient consequence for it to call for a unified concept, an intellectual attitude towards its component parts and consequently to the whole; and if there is a soloist, instrumental or vocal, to be accompanied. Most of all, the conductor ensures that one musical view prevails, ensemble players being notorious for their inability to agree on anything much beyond the union rate for the job.

A conductor's real work is done in rehearsal. During the first few minutes with a new man the players set out, often without pity, to discover whether or not the conductor knows his job.

'Maestro, should I have an E flat or an E natural nineteen bars after letter K?' they ask.

'Do you want an up-bow on the last quaver in bar 279?'

'Is the piccolo supposed to be in octaves with me at the third bar of the coda?'

The conductor hunts through his score, jabbing bars with his forefinger and suffering a sudden mental block over the transposition of the cor anglais or the exact meaning of *ausdrucksvoll*. He must keep his head; he must work steadily towards that unity of approach, that span of concept, which a serious symphonic work demands. He must also keep his temper (or lose it briefly and spectacularly), remember when to call the tea break, and not leave himself ten minutes at the end of rehearsal in which to get through a 35-minute work.

21

Then, some hours later when the evening concert begins, he has merely to remind the players with his gestures of the points that were established during the morning's rehearsal. This to a large extent leaves him free to entertain the paying customers; to offer them a focal point, a well-tailored back. In short, to put on a bit of an act.

And who doesn't? It is largely what the audience pays for. No one who has ever seen Sir George Solti conduct a concert would deny that in addition to being a master musician he is also a master showman. Those hypnotic eyes, the animal intensity—worth half the price of the ticket.

Again, when Rozhdestvensky momentarily decides to lay aside his conductor's baton and beam at his orchestra's efforts for a while without overt direction, it is worth a thousand pounds at the box office.

Some years ago, Leonard Bernstein, before acknowledging the audience's ovation at the end of Mahler's *Symphony of the Thousand*, raised the score solemnly to his lips and kissed it in homage. It was an unforgettable (if slightly *kitsch*) ending to a performance that had in a number of respects been memorable.

It's all part of the conductor's service. The luxuriant white locks and tapering fingers of Stokowski used to delight the eye every bit as much as his music rewarded the ear, sometimes even more. And how many of Sir Thomas Beecham's followers could lay their hands on their hearts and say that they never went to one of his concerts 'to see what the old devil will get up to next'?

Sir Thomas reached relatively early in life that enviable stage at which his mere presence in front of an orchestra would conjure from it a superior performance, such was the devotion, mingled with awe and respect, in which he was held. Other baton-wavers, commanding rather more respect than love, have only to glare at the second flute player for that individual to give the performance of his life through sheer terror. Most orchestral musicians of their day would rather have been hit on the head—literally—by Toscanini than patted on the cheek by Sargent. They knew a good thing when they saw it, and they learnt some new Italian words at the same time.

The authentic stars of the podium are men who feel the need for their contribution to music to be strongly physical as well as intellectual; active, self-willed men, with a didactic attitude to the gentle art of music. Some of them die young. The others seem to live on into a powerful old age, still masterminding a hundred men and women at a time, holding court in the world's luxury hotels and totting up conquests like the *Catalogue Song* in *Don Giovanni.*

Yet the view has been expressed by experienced labourers in the symphonic vineyard that by the time a conductor is about 80 years old he may have worked himself free of that initial compulsion to dominate men and win women, which brought him to fame, and be ready at last to serve Euterpe rather than a combination of Thespis and Eros. Given the repose of old age he will no longer fret about the cut of his dress jacket as seen from the back, but be prepared at long last to confine his attention to the composer's wishes as expressed in the score. Then, and perhaps only then (the theory goes), will he begin to approach that single-minded dedication to the great masters which their genius—and his—deserves. At 80 he is free at last of every consideration except the pursuit of pure art.

One who could surely be said to have reached that venerable and desirable stage was Dr. Otto Klemperer. At the age of 80 the formidable Klemperer, by then almost totally paralysed, would painfully mount the conductor's podium, transfix his players with that baleful eye which had known every great German musician from Mahler onwards, flex a finger by way of a starting signal, and simply stand there more or less motionless while the orchestra gave the performance of a lifetime of Beethoven's Seventh Symphony.

He did not direct; it was enough that he was present, and listening. As one of his horn players told me once, 'I have played Beethoven under Klemperer. What more is there to do?'

On the whole I tend to believe the charming anecdote about Klemperer and the trouser buttons, because it demonstrates the wonderful single-mindedness which becomes possible when God has allowed a specially favoured son to move into what footballers call 'extra time'.

One day, according to the story, the elderly Klemperer tottered onto the platform, stood for a moment in acknowledgment of the audience's welcome, then turned to the orchestra, perched on his conductor's stool—and unwittingly exposed an expanse of shirt through his open fly.

In vain the players tried to draw his attention to it. The hall was hushed . . . the symphony began . . . continued . . . developed . . . ended magnificently. At long last the orchestra leader managed to attract the old man's attention.

'Maestro,' he hissed, 'your fly buttons! They are undone!'

Klemperer regarded him with a mixture of disbelief and amazed contempt.

'Vot has dat to do wiz Beethoven?' he demanded.

My dear Pat, your choir conductor will not be a Klemperer, at least not yet. Being (I presume) younger, he will feel a strong desire to retain visible control over his choir at all times, even when he has launched you into a strict tempo, uniformly *mezzo-forte* passage which does not require any personal shaping or alteration, and all is going swimmingly.

A self-effacing conductor (and the words are almost contradictory) will admit, if only to himself, that for a good deal of the time he has nothing much to do and may as well not exert himself to disguise the fact from the world. At such moments his physical actions are of such little account that he might be well advised to take a leaf out of Rozhdestvensky's book, lay aside his baton, and stand back for a while to enjoy the music. If he is a born conductor his *presence*, rather than his gyrations, will determine the quality of the performance.

Tell me all about your choir's conductor. Is he a showman? A martinet? A menace? Is he *musical*?

And am I right: *are* you a little in love with him?

Yours

Steve

24

6

Dear Pat

I hope you understand that I had absolutely no idea you were engaged to him. I did not in any way mean to insult your fiancé. I'm sure he is a very good choir conductor. And how appropriate that you should have first noticed one another, in that personal sense, during a performance of Haydn's *Creation*!

I may have been guilty of suggesting a slight prejudice as between amateur and professional musicians when I wrote in my last letter about choir members and orchestral musicians. If so, I was over-compensating for a regrettable British tendency to regard professionalism as being somehow reprehensible, like the traditional distinction at Lord's Cricket Ground between Gentlemen and Players. ('*You* may play for money, my dear chap, *I* play for love.')

The distinction is not new. I came across a story told in 1642 by Thomas Fuller which illustrates it exactly. It seems that the Earl of Leicester, knowing that Queen Elizabeth delighted to see a gentleman dance well, brought the master of a dancing school before her for a demonstration.

A good idea? Not as it turned out. 'Pish,' said the queen. 'It is his profession. I will not see him.'

There it is in a nutshell. How superbly British—the man is

paid to do it, so I won't enjoy his expertise. (Remember Flanders and Swann's song of complaint about international athletic competitors who 'practise beforehand and ruin the fun'?) The cult of amateurism for its own sake is deeply ingrained in our national character; a prejudice which has been helped along in recent years by the popularity of such sayings as 'if a thing is worth doing at all, it's worth doing badly'.

It may well be so, but the fact is that it is even more worth doing *well*—and a little more likely to be done well by a full-time professional than by a part-time amateur.

The question of amateurs and professionals aside, I was most interested in your fiancé's views on the distinctions I made between the functions of orchestral and choral conductors. He is right, of course, to point out that some of the great conductors have excelled at both choral *and* orchestral work. On the other hand I would maintain that the ones the choir members admired most were hardly ever the players' favourites.

Quite apart from their normal professional or amateur status, singers and instrumentalists are different animals. Choir members are gregarious, regarding themselves as worker bees privileged to belong to a successful hive. All too often orchestral musicians regard themselves as more akin to a queen bee, condemned through some quirk of fate to ferry pollen to and fro until their unique qualities are recognized by the insensitive swarm. It has even been asserted that there is no such thing as a happy, fulfilled member of the second violins, least of all among the back desks.

Music is a hard taskmaster and sometimes a downright cruel profession. (Bizet called music 'a splendid art but a sad trade'.) It may well be that the greatest happiness is to be blessed with a modicum of talent. I am quite sure that the greatest misery is to be cursed with genius. Just ask Beethoven . . . or, for that matter, Charlie Parker or Janis Joplin. They knew that the world's rewards, such as they are, can be no compensation for the awful isolation that comes from being chosen by the gods to bear an enviable load of talent. 'Orpheus with his loot' (as the schoolboy had it) could find no cure for the 'care and grief of heart' that such people are condemned to carry.

Thank heaven one isn't a member of that club.

Yours

Steve

7

My Dear Pat

I feel sure you will accept my assurance that in referring in my last letter to 'Orpheus with his loot', I had absolutely no idea that your fiancé's name was Orpheus M. Pobjoy.

But how appropriate that his parents, having named him jointly after the legendary Greek musician and their favourite nineteenth-century composer, should live to see their son become the conductor of his own choir! The handbill you sent me for your choir concerts looks very imposing:

> The St. Anne's Singers—
> Musical director, conductor and artistic adviser
> Orpheus M. Pobjoy A.H.A.M.

I confess I had not realized until I read your letter that there even was a Huddersfield Academy of Music. But I look forward to the day when the name of Orpheus M. Pobjoy is on the lips of every musically informed person in the land, and Huddersfield duly takes its place beside Paris, Vienna, Bayreuth and Nashville.

Getting encouragement and a good musical start in life, as your Orpheus clearly did, is not by any means the destiny of every gifted artist. Orph (as you affectionately call him) will know the case of Thomas Arne in the eighteenth century, whose father expressly forbad him to practise any instrument for fear that it should make him want to enter the musical profession. As a result young Thomas Arne practised secretly on the violin and even on 'a muffled spinet'. In the end his father relented and allowed him to take up the art professionally . . . Which was a good thing, if only because the lad later wrote *Rule Britannia*, not to mention some lovely settings of Shakespeare. His own son, Michael—and one can't help wondering if he too in his turn was parentally deterred from taking up music as a profession—composed *The Lass with the Delicate Air*. Good chaps, the Arnes.

Little Mozart suffered from the opposite extreme, parentally speaking, being pushed and promoted by his father as pitilessly as any Hollywood moppet of the 1930s. A composer at the age of three, acclaimed as an international soloist at six, a mature composer of masses and symphonies, even operas, by the age of 12—poor Mozart! He was 'cursed with genius', as I put it in my last letter. By the age of 20 he was in a kind of relative retirement, lodged for the moment in Salzburg, hating his servile life as deeply as he loved his master, Music. What happiness he gave to the rest of us, and at what cost to himself!

On the matter of making a momentous start in life, consider the case of the Spanish composer, Albeniz. His astonishing public career began in 1864 when at only four years old he appeared as a solo pianist. Three years later, a mere seven, he applied for admission to the Paris Conservatoire, but was turned down. (Did they not see him, waiting his turn, behind the grand piano?) Undeterred, he toured Spain giving recitals, until at the grand old age of nine he took ship—on his own—to Cuba and America. There, in the absence of a guardian or manager, he fixed for himself an extensive concert tour.

Returning to Europe a hardened old pro of 13, Albeniz played briefly in London, studied for a while in Leipzig, then was offered at last a royal grant in his own country. He became a pupil of D'Indy and of Dukas (the *Sorcerer's Apprentice* man) and died, as one might almost have guessed he would, at an early age—only 48. At least the man had seen something of the world. What a ready-made interviewee for a television chat-show!

Saint-Saëns was another who gave remarkable early promise. Even as a tiny tot he showed that he possessed the phenomenon of absolute pitch, amazing everyone by being able to name notes as he heard them as well as to identify quite a wide range of musical pieces, all this before he was even three (we are told). The child was taken to be tested by a professor of music at the Paris Conservatoire, where he was made to stand facing a wall and asked to name a note which the professor played on the piano. He immediately did so.

'Wrong, my boy. You are a semitone out,' the professor reported, perhaps with a tinge of satisfaction. (Practitioners in an esoteric art do not greatly welcome infant prodigies.)

'No, sir, I am right!' persisted the little Saint-Saëns.

A tuning fork was brought. And it was then discovered that because of the piano's age and general condition the piano tuner had lowered all the strings by a semitone, but had neglected to mention it to the professorial staff.

Score: *1-nil* to the three-year-old. As for Professor Zimmerman, he is said to have resented that episode to the end of his life, as well he might. A little child shall lead them, as the Good Book says, but preferably not in the principal's room at the Paris Conservatoire.

As for clever little Saint-Saëns, he grew up and maintained that early promise. At the still tender age of 11 he gave a solo piano recital at the end of which, by way of an encore, he volunteered to play from memory any of Beethoven's 32 piano sonatas. (The boy seems to have had a gift for endearing himself to people of lesser abilities by quietly demonstrating how much lesser their abilities were.)

Nevertheless, great men practically queued up to admire him. Rossini took Saint-Saëns under his wing; Liszt offered praise; Gounod called him 'the French Beethoven', and Berlioz, wiser than the rest, commented quietly, 'He knows everything, but lacks experience.' (I find it strange to reflect that a man who knew Rossini lived to be on friendly terms with a man whom I later knew, Sir Arthur Bliss. Saint-Saëns seems

30

to condense almost two centuries into a single life span.)

As for Rossini, he (as everyone knows) did his composing early in life, got it safely accepted and then settled back in virtual retirement to enjoy the world's other pleasures. At 38, exactly half-way through his life—in fact a week or two after the première of *William Tell*—he simply opted out, devoting the rest of his life to being a wit and an epicure. He retired, wrote the perceptive critic Neil Hepburn, 'as any fat, lazy, apparently syphilitic and immoderately rich man with 39 operas behind him might reasonably be expected to do.' Exactly.

The large and languorous Rossini recognized in middle life that his bread was sufficiently buttered and jammed for him to take things easy thereafter. But he had always known where the jam was kept. On a visit to England at the age of only 29 he met all the Right People (including Lady Grenville, who described him as 'a fat, sallow squab of a man'). George IV took him to his heart, and evening after evening they made music together, the king himself performing as best he could at the piano.

Once King George apologized for his clumsy playing. Whereupon Rossini replied: 'Sir, there are few in your Royal Highness's position who could play so *well*', an impromptu comment which neatly steered a middle course between frankness and sycophancy.

Squab he may have been; diplomat he certainly was. So much so that on another occasion, when George IV asked him to select which item he would like the band to play, Rossini replied without a moment's hesitation. 'I would like to hear *God save the King*,' he said.

At the very opposite end of the spectrum from Rossini was César Franck, who composed virtually nothing of lasting musical interest until he was almost 60. Franck provides a cheering example to those of us who feel that somewhere inside us a great ninth symphony is lurking, even though we may not yet have managed to get the first eight down on paper. Your conductor fiancé may know that feeling, Pat. There will be times when 'Symphony in D minor, by Orpheus M. Pobjoy' may seem as remote to him as 'Symphony in D minor, by César

Franck' did to the 60-year-old organist at Sainte Clothilde.

Goodness, I do run on! But these composers' lives are fascinating, aren't they? 'So appallingly *human*,' as the old lady said. But, of course, that is why their music touches us.

Yours

Steve

8

Dear Pat

Yes, I did hear the world première broadcast performance of Carl Birdcage's *Monodic Lesions IX*. Like you, I found it rather hard to understand.

To begin with, the title wasn't much help, was it? I do wish Mr Birdcage would give his works plain English titles. Instead he follows the trend established a good many years ago by local born composers of the *avant-garde* persuasion, who suddenly started calling their creations *Canti Spectales*, *Contrapunctia III* or *Tetramorph for Brass Clusters*. (Even on the lighter side of music today's composers seem oddly drawn to titles like *Valse de la Jeunesse* and *Intermezzo Bacchanale*, though their creators are as English as steak and kidney pie.) Could it be that the old eighteenth-century prejudice still lingers: the conviction that only foreigners are any good at music? Or do our more earnest *avant-garde* young men court obscurity for its own sake? Perish the thought.

I have to confess that my understanding of Carl Birdcage's new work was not greatly helped by the explanatory notes read out by the radio announcer before the music began:

> The cyclic concept is based on inversionary infra-
> structures, whereby the main subject, or thematic

33

synthesis, is implied more by its absence than its presence. The element of *non-music* implicit in the structured silences emphasizes the composer's conceptual use of microtonal tension points . . .

No, I didn't quite understand that. Not for the first time I found the explanation harder to take than the work which it was supposed to illuminate. And I reflected again on how appropriate is the word 'work' in some musical contexts these days.

'Who wants music like that?' you ask bluntly, and the truthful answer is that (apart from the Arts Council) it is difficult to say. One feels like echoing the exasperated comment made by the Swiss composer, Honegger—whose own *garde* was pretty *avant* in its day—but who described such a composer as '. . . a kind of mad industrialist who persists in manufacturing an article nobody wants'. 'Nobody' in that context refers to the masses: people in general, the ordinary listener, the average concertgoer and record buyer.

So who supports such music? Answer: public funds. And should they? Answer: Yes, on the whole they should.

Consider another example: a new and excruciating ballet score which was premièred in the civilized city of Paris some years ago. The piece began with a strangulated cry from a bassoon, playing somewhat north of its comfortable range and suggesting that the young composer had little understanding of, or sympathy for, the art of orchestration. The music that followed was by turns opaque, clangorous and 'discordant'. After a minute or two the murmurs of irritation and disapproval turned to whistles, catcalls, even shouts of rage. The Austrian Ambassador, who happened to be present and knew a thing or two about music thanks to his shared nationality with Strauss, laughed out loud. The Comtesse de Pourtalés, a highly cultured musical lady whose presence at any major artistic event in Paris was what made it a major artistic event, left the auditorium abruptly, saying, 'I am 60 years old, but until now no one has dared to make a fool of me.'

The hapless composer, in the face of all this, had by now left the stalls and joined the ballet's producer in the wings who, poor fellow, furious at the mounting hubbub from the audience, was shouting out cues to the dancers, '16 . . . 17 . . .18 . . .' As the babel grew, the impresario who had commissioned the music ordered the electricians to flash the lights on and off in the hall in a vain effort to quell the riot.

Two members of the audience felt it their duty to make themselves heard in an attempt to silence the protesters. One was named Debussy, the other Ravel. For the occasion was, as I'm sure you've guessed, the first performance in 1913 of Stravinsky's *The Rite of Spring*, Nijinsky the producer, Diaghilev the impresario.

Now, Pat, ask yourself. Where were *you* sitting that night? Were you, as it were, the Comtesse de Pourtalés? Were you sneering, as Saint-Saëns was seen to do? Or were you, like Ravel, protesting that this was a work of genius that posterity would recognize as a turning point in the art of music?

Neither, I'm sure. You were sitting puzzled, hating the vulgar scene and the rabble, but nonplussed by the strangeness of the orchestral sound.

Great music that is also new music has always seemed strange at first. The difficulty is to know whether you are listening to a new *The Rite of Spring* or a new *Monodic Lesions IX* and, unfortunately, at a world première posterity is not there to tip you the wink.

Only one thing can be said for certain: if there had been no première of Stravinsky's alarming new ballet score the artistic world would have been an immeasurably poorer place. The Austrian Ambassador's hollow laugh rings still more hollowly down the decades. He and the Countess are an object lesson to every cloth-eared one of us—as I'm sure Carl Birdcage would be the first to point out, mistaking himself perhaps for a latter-day Stravinsky.

At all events, that is why the Arts Council and parallel bodies in other civilized countries spend their money, which is of course yours and mine, in commissioning young firebrands like Stravinsky and Birdcage to write the music that is in their hearts. One in a hundred, a thousand or, for all I know, one in a million of those works will be heard in the years to come, loved and reverenced by future generations whose ears are less hidebound than ours. Never forget the story of the two impresarios at the first play-through of a new musical work for the theatre, who jumped up in horror, one of them exclaiming, 'This isn't music!' Were they listening to *Moses und Aron*? *Lulu*? *The Bassarids*? No—it was *The Merry Widow*.

When I was a boy, old buffers used to relish telling us, 'Why, my grandchildren can paint as well as this fellow Picasso!' We know now how foolish they were. Nevertheless, it is irritating to be told that one's passionately held opinions may be proved wrong; that the evidence of one's own senses should be set aside in order to wait for the judgement of future generations: and all the more annoying when some of the *avant-garde* composers seem to be deliberately trying to test our credulity. They deceive us . . . Perhaps some of them even deceive themselves.

According to legend, a well known composer of difficult, cacophonous music walked into a concert hall one afternoon in order to listen to his latest creation being rehearsed by Sir Adrian Boult. Sitting in the stalls with ill-concealed impatience, the young man finally felt it necessary to interrupt the flow of strangulated sounds issuing from the orchestral players as they read the music before them and struggled to make sense of it.

'Sir Adrian,' cried the composer, 'Sir Adrian, excuse me a moment . . .'

'Oh Mr Blank, how nice to see you.' Sir Adrian, courteous as ever, gazed down into the body of the hall.

'Sir Adrian, do forgive me, but couldn't you take it just a *little* bit quicker?' asked the young composer.

'Indeed we could, Mr Blank. But you do realize, don't you, that we haven't come to your piece yet?'

Musicians enjoy telling stories like that, especially those who habitually deal in more readily accessible music. There is no doubt that a lot of difficult new music is simply pointless; a confidence trick, if you like. Yet what is the young composer to do? He must write music that is 'new' because these days he cannot make his mark writing stylistically 'old' music.

I remember being present in a lecture hall when a panel of musical experts was being asked questions from the floor.

'I have a question,' said a young woman sitting near me. 'It's this. If a young composer in our own day wrote a score *in the style of Handel and as fine as Handel*, would it be published? Would it be acclaimed?'

'Oh yes,' replied the panel of experts with one voice. 'Oh yes. Certainly.'

But they spake not the truth, and I suspect they knew it. No new music these days written in the straightforward harmonic idiom of Handel's time would be accepted for serious performance by any organization I have ever come across, unless the work were an intentional pastiche, or purported to have been dictated direct from Handel himself by occult means. New music, to be welcomed by the musical establishment, must *sound* new.

Don't ask me why, Pat. In this peculiarity music seems to be the odd man out among the arts. Representational painters still flourish; poets may write in the style of Rupert Brooke and still be published; novelists produce Jane Austen sequels; potters make neo-classical ash trays. It all comes down to the vital question of *idiom* . . . The manner of speech, the dialect, that one chooses in order to put across one's personal creative message. I repeat: new music these days, to be officially acceptable, must for some reason be couched in the language of novelty.

There is more to be said about that. But not now, not now! My apologies for going on almost as long as Carl Birdcage did in his *Monodic Lesions IX*. I shall be interested to hear what your fiancé Orpheus thought about the piece.

Yours

Steve

37

9

My Dear Pat

I was quite saddened by your last letter. It was obvious that you greatly admired your fiancé Orpheus as a conductor and choirmaster, as well as feeling affection for him as a person. I had imagined that your relationship with him was progressing happily, or at any rate smoothly. Now that you have told me about his philandering, though, I realize (as you do) that you are well rid of such a man. And to desert you for a contralto almost twice his age!

Small wonder that you have resigned from his choir. Carl Orff's *Catulli Carmina* would have been fun to take part in, I agree, but you are well rid of such a two-timer. No doubt Orpheus will now be privately coaching his contralto friend in some of the work's trickier bits of timing. Try not to think about it.

To tell the truth, I was never quite sure that Orpheus was the right man for you. In the snapshot you sent me from Bognor I noticed that he was somewhat shorter in height than you are, despite his platform soles. I confess to having a quite unjustifiable suspicion of men who use a tiepin to secure the collar-tabs under their ties, prudent though it may be. I am sure that someone as young (and may I say as attractive?) as yourself will very soon find another escort; perhaps one a little

38

taller, too.

Meanwhile there is music to be enjoyed, is there not? You ask point blank in your letter how you can make yourself like *avant-garde* music and my immediate reply is that perhaps you should not try. If, inevitably, some form of music fails to please you I cannot think of any reason why you should beat your brains out trying to get on terms with it.

This is not quite the same thing as being comfortably insular and unadventurous in your artistic tastes. I would not be the one to recommend that. I am simply suggesting that every intelligent listener has a sticking point, and that sometimes it is pointless to push too hard at a closed door, particularly if one has doubts as to whether undiscovered riches really do lie on the other side.

What exactly is the problem with 'new' music? I am inclined to think that *harmony* is the element in music which separates questing listeners from an understanding of unfamiliar sounds, rather than *rhythm* or *melody*. Let me explain. To back-track first: I'm sure you know that all music—or all our western music, at any rate—is made up of three elements: melody, harmony and rhythm. Take them separately.

Melody is the tune, the air; the thing that most of us enjoy most in music. Melody doesn't have to be succulent, slow or 'tuneful'—even *The Flight of the Bumble Bee* is a melody, albeit a rapid one.

Harmony exists whenever more than one musical tone is heard simultaneously. Again, it isn't necessary for it to be rich or 'harmonious': that would be to add a value judgement to a mere technicality, though it is true that harmonies richer or more complex than simple hymnbook favourites remain beyond the appreciation of a great many people. Harmony tends to separate, as they say, the men from the boys.

Rhythm is what gives momentum to music, and it exists the moment one note gives place to another, since by that simple change an instant has been struck in time. There is also the rhythm of a different kind that comes from the deliberately regular spacing out of time, as in marches, jazz and pop music. The proper word for that is not so much rhythm as *pulse*.

39

Most of us these days are inured to music which seems to lack melody and we do not object to its temporary absence if the pulse is attractive enough. One can dance or drive—some youngsters would say one can study for exams, too—to a background of music consisting almost exclusively of pulse. One either likes or doesn't like the sort of pulse-rhythm that gives jazz and pop music its throbbing character.

Do I hear a small voice saying that all this theorizing is of no help when you are battling with the incomprehensibility of Carl Birdcage's latest opus? (Opus 159b, I notice. How like the *avant-garde* boys that is!) What are you to listen for? Melody? Harmony? Rhythm?

The chances are that you will find it hard to identify any of those ingredients, or rather determine any logic in the way he has used them. In the strictly technical sense, melody, harmony and rhythm are present in virtually all music. But the first rule is to give the composer the benefit of the doubt. He *is* sincere, he *does* mean it, he *does* have a message for you. Begin with that thought . . . then listen to what the man has to say.

In order to get his message across the composer has chosen a particular musical idiom, in this instance rather an intractable one. But at least he has faced up to the creative artist's deepest problem. He has asked himself, 'Who am I?' And he has found an answer.

Even this is by no means as easy as it sounds. The choice of a musical language is absolutely central to the beginning of any worthwhile creative musical act, and the more gifted the musician, the more skilful he is, the harder that choice will be for him.

Take it from me, there are any number of clever musicians around who can write convincingly in almost any style asked of them. I can think of a score of workaday musician friends of mine—musical directors, TV conductors, jingle composers and arrangers—who could write briefly and successfully in almost any given style. Say to them, 'Write me 16 bars of a Handel aria, half a page of a Beethoven symphony, or the first phrase of a Gershwin song,' and they will do just that. The work these skilful music men produce could fool almost anyone for a moment, though it has to be added that a *lengthy* Handel aria, an entire movement of a Beethoven symphony or even a full 32-bar Gershwin chorus would be quite another matter. The problem my competent musical friends face occurs not when they are commissioned to produce a chunk of pseudo-Rachmaninov, but when a voice utters the dread words 'be yourself'.

What then? Where are their creative powers to feed? How to begin? 'Right,' they say, 'I am about to compose a serious piece of music. Now—who shall I be? What style shall I write in? *Who am I?*'

I don't believe any truly great composer ever had to ask himself that question. The young Mozart never needed to decide whether to write in the style of Gluck, Haydn or Bach. He simply took pen in hand and started to write, painfully perhaps, and with great travail, though somehow in his case I doubt it. He knew who he was and what he had to do. His fiercely individual spirit dictated the idiom we know as Mozartian.

To take another example from nearer our own time, Edward Elgar wrote in the style of Edward Elgar almost from the first moment he picked up a pencil and doodled some musical notes on a stave. No one had quite caught it before; no one need trouble to attempt it again. There stands the utterly individual music of Elgar: pointless to imitate it, unthinkable to ignore it.

The question of identity is perhaps the one problem that never really troubles the truly great, indeed that is what makes them great, whether their names be Scarlatti, Stravinsky or Sondheim. What I am talking about is the ultimate gift, and it may illustrate why composers find it so amazingly difficult to explain their methods and creative processes. Elgar probably thought he was being quite helpful when he wrote for the benefit of us lesser folk that 'music is in the air: you sim 'y take as much of it as you want'. When pressed for further i. orma-tion as to where music really came from, he obligingly tried again. 'The trees are singing my music,' he said. 'Or have I sung theirs?'

41

What did Brahms have to say about the source of music? While working on a symphony he wrote, 'So many melodies fly around here that one has to be careful not to tread on them!' Much earlier, my beloved William Byrd had tried to explain the same happy experience. 'The right notes, in some strange manner,' he reported, 'come of their own accord to the wakeful and expectant mind.' To him, no doubt, they did. A less enthusiastic note was sounded by Sir William Walton in his seventies. 'Composing,' he said, 'has never come easily to me, and the older I get the more difficult it seems to become. I seriously advise all sensitive composers to die at the age of 37.' It was a Waltonianism; he didn't mean it.

To return to Carl Birdcage and his *Monodic Lesions IX*, I feel we have no alternative but to concede that the man is sincerely trying to tell us something, even though his language may be woefully, even wilfully, unfamiliar to us. No doubt we could have required him to communicate in the common language of accepted tonal music, but that is not the idiom in which he chooses to work or (as I have explained) that the musical establishment is prepared to accept. To do so might have cost him his sponsorship.

Let me try to be practical on how you might approach his piece once more.

First of all, don't look for anything so familiar as a theme and subsequent variations. Don't look for the time-honoured first and second subjects, development, recapitulation and coda form, so dear to commentators on the classical sonata or symphony. In fact don't look for melody at all. Don't look for familiar recognition points, nor for structure. There may be a structural form of some sort but it is unlikely to be apparent in so unfamiliar a setting.

Try listening to the harmony. Does it offer tension and release? Harmony almost always does. To take a much loved example, check the love theme from Tchaikovsky's *Fantasy Overture, Romeo and Juliet*, and notice how at almost every point there is tension between the tune and its accompaniment (for example on the very first note of the tune), while within the accompaniment that yearning counter-melody played on the horn is constantly tightening and loosening. Harmony is concerned with conveying a feeling of tension and release and our young progressive friend, Carl Birdcage, has at least inherited that from his predecessors. Or has he only inherited tension? At least try him.

Rhythm, in the sophisticated sense or even in the plain sense of pulse, does not seem to be what Carl Birdcage is concerned with, being more involved in *space*: 'temporal space' I have heard it called. So try an experiment on his terms, and let his music take over your time sense for a while. You may find yourself suddenly won over, because what he is seeking to do is to *touch* you, to reach you. And that, come to think of it, is exactly what Haydn and Holst, Beethoven and Britten sought to do, though in their less forbidding musical language.

Back to Birdcage, my dear Pat: give him another chance. I see his piece is being repeated on the radio later this week. Let's try him again, shall we?

Your affectionate

Steve

10

My Dear Pat

No, I didn't enjoy it either, though I did try to listen in a co-operative frame of mind. There was a moment about twenty minutes from the start when I felt that Mr Birdcage wanted me to feel sleepy. Taking my cue from him, I closed my eyes in order to assist in the experiment—and the next thing I knew the radio announcer was telling me that Schubert was 19 when he wrote his Fifth Symphony. I gathered that we had moved on to the next item in the programme.

I don't really agree with your well-intentioned suggestion that more attention to the programme notes might have helped us. How did that passage go again? 'The cyclic concept is based on inversionary techniques . . . Structured silences . . . Microtonal tension points . . .'

No. In contrast I cannot help recalling that when the admirably practical composer Malcolm Arnold was invited to contribute an explanatory programme note for one of his specially commissioned works premièred at the Royal Albert Hall, he wrote (as I remember), 'I had a lot of pleasure writing this. I hope you enjoy listening to it.' That was all he said.

Perhaps we have spent long enough trying to get in touch with *Monodic Lesions IX*, you and I. Despite its unenticing name, maybe it will get to us in due course.

A funny thing about titles: the more serious and important the work, the less attention seems to be given to what it should be called. I am sure Delius laboured long and lovingly over naming his slight but lovely *To be Sung on a Summer Night on the Water* or the orchestral reverie *On Hearing the First Cuckoo in Spring*. But it's odd: when Mendelssohn takes his turn at writing a watery, spring-like piece, the best he seems able to manage is *Lieder ohne Worte No. 12, opus 30, No. 6: Venetianisches Gondellied in F sharp minor*. Not very liquid!

Brahms, too. A single man, he wrote a letter to a young lady of his acquaintance enclosing his latest compositions and asking, 'Will you permit me to put your honoured name, in dedication, to these humble and inadequate pieces of rubbish? And can you think of a better title than *Two Rhapsodies for Pianoforte?*'

One would have thought almost anybody could think of a better title than that. I wonder sometimes if the lady felt like replying, 'Thanks for the compliment, but why don't you call them *Homage to a Divine Face*, or *Ecstasy, thy name is Elisabeth von Herzogenberg?*'

What she actually wrote in reply was: 'You gave me real joy by sending me these splendid pieces . . . I note their lovely curves and windings and their wonderful ebb and flow. Although the G minor is my favourite, I fully appreciate the strong pungent beauty of the other . . .' Clearly the girl knew just how to write to a composer. She uttered no word of complaint about the unromantic title, reflecting I suppose that if a composer doesn't know at 47 how to treat a beautiful girl (even one called Elisabeth von Herzogenberg) he never will. 'I welcome to my heart,' she concluded bravely, 'these nameless ones in the misty robes of Rhapsodies!'

No doubt it could be claimed that great artists are deliberately casual about the titles of their works because they regard the label as being infinitely less important than the contents. Shakespeare, after all, saddled some of his plays with names that are not so much an exercise in titling as in opting out of making a tiresome decision: *Much Ado about Nothing, As You Like It, What You Will* . . . The titles tell us deliberately next to nothing about the setting, cast or content of the play. One can only conclude that the playwright did not want the audience to approach the performance with any preconceived ideas.

That is certainly the intention when Beethoven completes a deeply moving piano piece and writes soberly across the title page, '*Sonata quasi una fantasia*, op. 27, No. 2.' Significantly, it was not the composer but a later music critic who observed that Beethoven's piece reminded him of moonlight on Lake Lucerne.

The idea caught on, and most of us think of the first movement anyway as simply Beethoven's *Moonlight Sonata*; though if you met the composer in Valhalla and mentioned his *Moonlight Sonata* he would not know which of his works you meant. He might even think you meant the slow movement of his *Sonata Pathétique*, op. 13, for that too has something of the stillness of a moonlit lake, and with a pleasing top-dressing of ripples.

The nickname 'moonlight' was the brainchild of one Rellstab, whose name always strikes me as being either some obscure code word or conceivably an anagram on his real name, L. Blaster. It was left to a great nineteenth-century pianist, Anton Rubinstein, to point out that, even if the scene could be described as moonlit, the music undoubtedly tells of 'a sky covered with heavy leaden clouds'.

The same piece was sometimes known in Vienna under yet another nickname: the *Arbour Sonata*, the composer having reportedly written it while sitting in an arbour. But earlier still, in fact in Beethoven's own time, yet another story had got about.

This told how on one of his solitary walks in the countryside the composer had met a young blind girl. Without recognizing who he was, she confided to him that above all other music she loved that of Herr Ludwig van Beethoven, and her dream was that just once in her life she would meet the master and he would play for her. Much moved (so the story goes), Beethoven led her back to his home, and there—sitting in a shaft of moonlight—he improvised his C sharp minor Sonata for the poor blind girl. The shaft of moonlight could only have been reported by Beethoven himself, since the girl could not see it. But in any case the story smacks more of a Charlie Chaplin scenario than a real life experience. What we know for certain about the *Moonlight Sonata* is that it was dedicated to Countess Giulietta Guicciardi, in Beethoven's words 'an adorable young girl'.

And why this particular sonata? The answer seems to be somewhat less than romantic. The composer had already dedicated to her a rondo which for a variety of reasons he wanted back; mainly he wanted it returned in order to re-dedicate it to Princess Lichnowsky. So to get the rondo back from the adorable Giulietta he dedicated the C sharp minor Sonata to her instead.

He added the words '*quasi una fantasia*' to the more formal description of sonata in order to justify its lack of the customary first movement form. Perhaps also—who knows?—in an attempt to discourage sentimentalists from reading into it romantic stories like the one about the blind girl in the moonlight. We shall never know his true thoughts, though one of his pupils (Czerny), who may well have played the work in his presence, called it 'a nocturne in which spectral voices are heard lamenting in the distance'. Did that thought come originally from Beethoven? It just might have done. But again, we shall never know.

That first and most popular movement of the *Moonlight Sonata* is often played as if it were a funeral march, though Beethoven would have given it a very different tempo marking from *adagio* if he had really wanted it to be performed at graveyard pace. In a similar connection, a great Chopin exponent, Alfred Cortot, observed sharply that 'as a man Chopin may have been ill, but his music should not be played as if someone were dying'. Exactly. The pianist who seeks to interpret the *Moonlight Sonata* should not (to adapt Stevie Smith's poem) seem to be drowning, just gently waving.

The days when famous pianists drowned in emotion at their recitals are now more or less ended, though reports still linger of Maestro X turning his tear-stained face to the audience, and Maestro Y having to go off and rest for some minutes between movements of the *Waldstein*. A few pianists may still survive who play a note *espressivo* and then waggle their finger from side to side as if to add vibrato, though they must know perfectly well that it cannot possibly affect the sound, which is already launched (indeed dying away).

I have a feeling that Liszt may have been a finger-waver. He certainly did everything else to make his recitals romantically effective and memorable, and those who were privileged to see him in action never forgot the experience.

'I was carried away by the sweetness of his expression,' wrote the novelist George Eliot, a lady who noticed men, and a fan if ever Liszt had one. 'Genius, benevolence and tenderness beamed from his whole countenance. As he played, for the first time in my life I beheld real inspiration. There was nothing strange or excessive about his manner. His manipulation of the instrument was quiet and easy. But his face was utterly grand, the lips compressed, the head thrown a little backwards. When the music denoted quiet rapture or devotion, a sweet smile flitted across his features. When it was *triumphant*, the nostrils dilated.'

You almost feel yourself there! But 'quiet and easy' were not the words that came into the mind of another enraptured member of Liszt's audience.

'As the closing strains began, I saw Liszt's countenance assume an agony of expression mingled with radiant smiles of joy. His hands rushed over the keys, the floor shook like a wire and the whole audience was wrapped with sound. Then—the frame of the artist gave way. He fainted into the arms of a friend who had been turning over the pages for him, and was borne out in a strong fit of hysterics. The whole room sat still, breathless with fear, until it was announced from the platform that Liszt was restored to consciousness and was comparatively well again.'

Note the word 'comparatively', Pat. Not well enough to come back and complete the recital perhaps, but well enough to go out and consume a light dinner. Incidentally, I do think we might spare a thought across the intervening century for the 'friend who had been turning the pages': one moment trying to anticipate the master's forward-reading ability, the next moment receiving his prostrate form, trying to disengage Liszt's feet from the pedals and hauling him off into the wings for resuscitation.

No performer, even of Liszt's standard, ought to 'faint into the arms of a friend' in the middle of a recital unless, of course, he has suddenly learnt that the box office has been the subject of an armed raid. That eventuality reminds one of the scene which took place once in Beethoven's dressing-room after a performance of his ninth symphony.

The impresario who had mounted the concert went backstage, taking with him a copy of the attendance figures. As he himself reported it: 'I handed the composer a note of the ticket office receipts for the evening, and Beethoven collapsed at the sight of them. We stayed at his side till late at night; he asked for no food or drink, and did not speak. Finally, on perceiving him asleep, we went quietly away. His servant found him next morning exactly as we had left him, asleep, and still in the clothes in which he had conducted.'

Shock box-office figures apart, the solo performer is concerned with the well judged transmission of emotion, not with indulging in it himself. To a degree it could be claimed that the one includes the other. But no one playing, say, the gorgeous slow movement of Dvorak's cello Concerto would dare to allow himself the luxury of a lachrymose moment, lest a tear should fall on the fingerboard just at the very moment when the double-stoppings are demanding the player's fullest attention.

To sway or not to sway? To emote or not to emote? A completely dry, inert approach to a musical performance will not even fill the gallery with people, still less the boxes, and the recitalist must accept the fact, however dedicated he may be. Audiences go to a live concert in order to *see* music being played. If they wanted only to hear it, they would stay at home with the radio or join a gramophone society.

The sheer mechanics of playing an instrument—be it piano, violin, flute or human voice—place certain limitations on the performer's physical gestures, though beyond those limitations there lies a wide range of choice, ranging from gentlemanly concern to manifest torture. Most musicians find a comfortable compromise quite early in their careers between extravagant emotionalism and an uncommunicating stillness. Weaving and deep breathing, though, tend to grow over the years rather than to diminish.

Few successful solo artists could draw from a critic the particular praise that Deems Taylor gave to Wilhelm Backhaus, in the days when rampant pianistic lions roamed the concert halls, terrifying the shades of composers no less than their audiences.

'Backhaus has no mannerisms or platform tricks,' observed Deems Taylor. 'He keeps his hands on the keyboard and his mind on the music. He does not make faces or crack small jokes with the audience. He falls into no sculpturesque poses. Some of his hair is long, but more of it is missing. And the present scribe, who has been mistaken for him on occasion, is one of the few persons who are strikingly impressed by his personal beauty.'

That passage speaks volumes for Backhaus, and incidentally for the critic who wrote it, too.

Very different from . . . Well, Beethoven for one. As a pupil of his reported afterwards, 'He insisted on a light touch. But he himself was often violent, throwing the music around and tearing it up.' Even the devoted Pleyel admitted that 'he has great fire, but he pounds a bit too much'.

If then performers should on the whole be still, what about audiences?

'It is the custom in this country, when a lady or gentleman happens to sing, for the company to sit as mute and motionless as statues. Every feature, every limb, must seem to correspond in fixed attention, and while the song continues they are to remain in a state of universal petrifaction.' So wrote Oliver Goldsmith, commenting (in the guise of a visiting foreigner) on the London audience of his eighteenth century.

My preference is for the performer to be reasonably still and the audience utterly so, at any rate while the music is being played. I am for what another eighteenth-century writer called 'the quiet composure of the body', though on the subject of

50

applause *between movements* I hold heretical views which I must leave for another letter. This one has gone on quite long enough!

Your affectionate

Steve

11

My Dear Pat

Your new boy friend sounds most interesting, even though you only mention him as a kind of afterthought. Half a line in the PS! From his name I take him to be a trumpet or cornet player; unless he, like his namesake the immortal Bix Beiderbecke, was originally christened Bismarck, which seems unlikely these days (though after Orpheus not impossible). Whatever the origin of his name, Bix sounds like rather a different person from Orpheus.

To quote your PS: 'My new boy friend, Bix, says he is "into mainstream". Naturally, I would like to be into it too, whatever it is. Can you tell me please—what is it?'

You've come to the right person, my dear, as Sweeney Todd used to say. But be warned: this is a jazz question, and jazz is a subject on which no two people hold the same opinion. It therefore follows that on this topic anyone's opinion is as good as anyone else's. You shall have mine.

When the jazz story comes to be told in full—when every critic, commentator, discographer and social historian has had his say—there will be seen to have been basically five kinds of instrumental jazz. I would call them classic, mainstream, modern, free-jazz and jazz-rock. The possible subdivisions are endless, but those five will do as basic headings.

52

Classic jazz began when and where jazz itself began: the turn of the century, Africa and New Orleans. It developed from a fusion (or, more properly, *con*fusion) of Wesleyan missionary hymns and tribal rhythms, with some of the would-be gentility of the bordello thrown in, thanks to the influence of ragtime.

Ragtime was for indoors, jazz for out. So on the streets of New Orleans, where fun and noise belonged, the marching musician learnt his rags, blues and marches, making up any bits he couldn't quite remember, weaving an exuberant impromptu counter-melody when he found the man next to him playing the same tune, competing in embellishments. In short, having fun.

If he was a cornet player he carried the main tune, being the owner of the boldest instrument on the street. If a trombonist, he honked out some sort of makeshift harmony-cum-bass-line, often sliding between the notes (as trombones can) because making a healthy vulgar noise attracted the attention of the laughing girls on the sidewalk. If he was a clarinettist he ripped off impressive florid passages which his brass-playing rivals, in the very nature of their instruments, could not execute. Drummers, banjoists, guitarists and brass-bass men thumped away enthusiastically in support.

It must have sounded like John Philip Sousa's band on an off day.

Improvising noisy music in the open air is a barrel of fun if you can't play your instrument very well, but a bit frustrating if you can. One unremembered day, someone—a star cornettist perhaps, or a more than usually nimble-fingered clarinet player—made a brief speech.

'Look, you guys,' he said. 'I'm tired of having to battle against you lot all the time. Knock it off for a minute, and give me a solo turn.' At that moment the story of jazz turned another page.

Classic jazz, in the broadest possible terms, meant New Orleans-based marching music in which the wind players, working together as an ensemble, stated a chosen tune and wove their embellishments around it. But now the era of the soloist had begun.

53

The basic process had not changed, only the emphasis on the individual. Now, when Louis Armstrong took his solo turn on *Basin Street Blues*, the new melody he created was no longer a perceptible extension of the original tune. A great improvisatory revolution had taken place.

The root of the operation, the underlying framework that had kept both the soloist's and the listener's place in the music, was no longer the melody. Now it was the chord sequence, and so it has remained through most of the subsequent jazz story.

It is the *chords* of the song which the jazz soloist has running through his mind as he improvises, not its melody. He creates an entirely new tune over the memorized sequence of chords.

Ask any jazz musician if he'll jot down *Basin Street Blues* for you, and the chances are that he will write, not melody notes on a musical stave, but something purely hieroglyphic that begins: B♭ / D7 / G7 / G7 / . . .

Jazz musicians the world over need only a one-line sequence of letters and digits in order to pump out variations on the chords of *Basin Street Blues*, if necessary for hours, with a chorus or two of the tune front and rear to set the thing off. They may not know a word of one another's spoken language but their musical *rapport* will be complete.

This was the first major revolution in jazz. No longer were its practitioners merely decorating a house; they were building a completely new one on earlier foundations. Some people complained that in the change the authenticity and decorative purpose of the old jazz had been lost. Many listeners, having no great taste for harmony or instinct for harmonic sequence, no longer knew where they were in the music once the original melody had disappeared. It was understandable. At every stage of artistic development somebody opts out.

By the 1930s the mainstream jazzmen would state the composer's original tune rather cursorily for 32 bars, then take off on their imaginative flights. This was almost total freedom, for now the only thing that constrained the improvising musician was a broad allegiance to the basic chord structure. Beyond that he was as free as air, like a racing motorist who can vary his strategy, but only in terms of the circuit he is riding.

At this stage some brilliantly creative performers took the centre of the jazz stage: people like the tenor saxophonist, Coleman Hawkins, and the great Duke Ellington soloists. Dig out from that period any record of, say, *Body and Soul* or *Perdido*, and after the routine opening statement of the tune you will find little trace of it again until the end of the record. What one hears instead is impromptu playing, often of an astonishingly high order.

Jazz, and jazz alone, revived the lost art of impromptu music making (except for certain folk cultures, where it has never failed to exist). The excitement of hearing—still more of making—instant music, is tremendous. Many of us owe our interest in the jazz movement to that fact. One remains dumbfounded at the numbers of jazz addicts, including famous critics and authorities on the subject, who seemingly have never felt the compulsion to try to play jazz and find out how it feels to do it oneself.

Those were the days of the great 'jam session' musicians, whose creative freemasonry could take them into a jazz cellar in Tokyo, Texas, Tunis or Tyneside, safe in the knowledge that a simple code-word like *Undecided, Shine* or *Margie* would produce an instant 30-minute free-for-all in a universally accepted key, with every musician in turn contributing. Happy, heady days those were, for those who shared the secret.

But anything so relatively simple could never be sufficiently challenging for the younger, questing jazz musicians; a new wave of rebels led by Charlie Parker in the 1940s. The revolutionary movement which they inaugurated—I am calling it modern jazz for the purposes of this brief history—offered the soloist a new and greater freedom.

He was still committed to working over a basic 12 or 32-bar sequence of chords. But, in order to challenge his own inventiveness, the player set about making the chords more intricate and sophisticated, the themes more chromatic. A new repertoire of 'standard' numbers grew up, many of them originally show songs but with interesting harmonic progressions, like *How High the Moon* or *I'll Remember April*. There were new and exciting freedoms within the extended rules, and the young post-war jazzmen were quick to learn them.

Again there were those who could not go along with the new sounds. And there were others who wanted to go much further; the ones who find any discipline at all irksome. About the year 1970 anarchy arrived in the shape of free-jazz, in which a handful of musicians started making up music simply as it came into their heads: no guidelines, no rules, no holds barred. An aural scribble on a blank sheet.

This time *I* was among those who moved out, protesting that where there are no ground rules the game is not worth playing, still less going to watch. By definition no one (including the musicians) knew what the free-jazz exponents were doing, indeed *not* knowing was the whole point of their efforts.

Doubtless for them it brought therapeutic release; for the listener it had about as much point as an endless football match with no lines, no goals, no rules, no referee and no score. Not to mention a very small supporters' club.

It goes without saying that while jazz was going through its developmental stages, so was everything else within range. Popular music, protesting against the effete, musicianly sounds that the professional dance musicians had wished on the public in the Thirties and Forties, exploded in the mid-Fifties with rock 'n' roll.

Looking back from the point of view of a professional working musician at the time, the only thing that now surprises me about rock is that its coming was so long delayed. Instead of the old musical sophistication epitomized by the Glenn Miller sound—smoochy, smoothly organized—it offered a new raw simplicity, under a catchy name that was hard, aggressive, and not too difficult to spell.

We, the popular music dispensers in the dance bands, had had it our own way for so long, pretending to give the simple, undemanding public what it wanted, while in reality we were merely indulging our taste for clever harmonies and ingenious tricks of orchestration; coupled, of course, with the dance musician's fondness for improvised jazz, which we would knock out for a few bars whenever we dared, while the public sat back, puzzled, wondering where the tune had gone.

It took someone as commercially purposeful as Bill Haley to strip away the self-indulgent jazz solos and the effete murmurings of sentimental swing, offering the new public what in all probability the *old* public had long wanted: a brazen, pounding beat, plain repetitive words, and to hell with the harmonies.

Rock itself settled down after a while and before long was becoming increasingly sophisticated within its own rugged terms; the pendulum always swings back if you let a little time go by. But by then a number of interesting spin-off developments were affecting jazz, thanks to the arrival of electrically amplified instruments.

The guitar, double-bass and piano—the very instruments which throughout their jazz careers had found it virtually impossible to make themselves heard—were now, in contrast, the loudest instruments in the band. And the band itself was smaller. No longer were a dozen or more men needed to fill a dance hall with sound. A couple of guitarists and a drummer could practically bring down Carnegie Hall, given a good sound system . . . or even a bad one.

Most musically-minded youngsters took to pop music. But a few needed the added creative stimulus that jazz-based improvisation alone could provide.

So a new hybrid was born, and a highly stimulating one too: jazz-rock. It combined the instant creative challenge of modern jazz with the electronic revolution that had come with rock, the whole thing backed up by a pounding beat of exciting power and considerable complexity. It was the natural channel of expression for a youngster who found conventional jazz too insipid but rock too blatant. He fused the two, to make a genuinely new form.

So there it is, Pat: my hopelessly synoptic dash through the hundred years or so of jazz development: classic jazz to jazz-rock in five relatively painful stages.

From his nickname I would guess that your friend Bix is a trumpet player involved in the fringe area between the first and second of those Five Ages of Jazz, using the old Twenties'

57

standard tunes like *There'll be some Changes Made* and *That's a Plenty* as the basis for his improvisations, but working on the stimulus of the chords during his solos rather than on the original tunes, hence Bix's claim to be 'into mainstream'. As he and his friends will know, improvising on a set of chords is a good deal harder to do than mere tune-embroidering, but it is more rewarding for those who can manage it.

Browning said (though I admit he wasn't talking about jazz at the time) that 'a man's reach should exceed his grasp'. Or what, demanded the poet, 'is a heaven for?'

The 'heaven' that your young friend Bix will reach out for as his technical abilities develop will be something nearer to the heading of modern jazz than of mainstream, I suspect. The jazz world is full of instrumentalists who began with techniques as limited as those of the pioneer jazzmen whom they so revere, but who spread their stylistic wings as their execution improves. No musician ever seems to move in the opposite direction, backwards in jazz time.

Early jazz can indeed be something of a straitjacket. Its legendary founders spent their whole working lives playing in only two or three keys. Their entire musical output was in four-time. And it was played at every volume level from *ff* to *fff*.

People like me, who have grown a shade tired of jazz, have done so because of those limitations. Jazz *is* appallingly limited in terms of key and time signatures. It is almost always played too loudly for there to be any subtlety of nuance, especially now that the jazz musician feels threatened by the popularity of deafening rock music.

I love the occasional sound of a genuine pioneer jazz band. But just because Hot-lips Henriques spent 50 years of his life blowing *Dippermouth Blues* very loudly in the key of B flat (and usually fairly sharp) is no reason why less limited players should not make an effort to embrace broader forms, more varied keys, more challenging time signatures and some semblance of dynamic variety.

Worthwhile music deserves care and thought in performance. Even the heavenly creations of a Mozart, if played in the

58

same key and uniformly *double-forte*, would soon pall. Music's reach should exceed its grasp, as Browning said.

Where does your Bix stand on all this, I wonder? Have you heard him play yet? And does he sound like Bix Beiderbecke?

Your affectionate

Steue

12

My Dear Pat

So your friend Bix is a drummer. My mistake. I'm glad you think he is a good one and have been enjoying his jazz group's rehearsals in the upstairs room at the Dog and Rabbit. How surprised the trophies of the Royal Antediluvian Order of Buffaloes must be!

If history is repeating itself—and it usually does, I've noticed—you may be feeling slightly divided in your mind over those rehearsal sessions, interesting and often exciting though those jazz-filled hours can be for members of the supporters' club. Jazz musicians' girl friends can find themselves spending a great deal of their time chatting perfunctorily to jazz musicians' girl friends, while their menfolk send out for refills of cider and explore ever more deeply the amazing chord sequence of *I Got Rhythm*. (Not unlike life for rugby widows, though at least your man won't come back from a practice session with his teeth kicked in.)

One of the early Quaker rules declared music to be 'unnecessary', on account of 'the noise it makes and the time it takes'. You may have entertained similar thoughts during the seventh trombone chorus of *Creole Love Call*. Not that long improvised trombone solos are the hardest to take. Oh no. That honour belongs jointly to the bass player and (saving your

Bix's efforts) the drummer.

I can recall a time in jazz when neither the bassist nor the drummer was thought to have any claim whatever on the solo time available. Their job was to keep the rhythm going, the bass player with an unwavering four-in-a-bar broadly based on the harmonies, while the drummer beat time, with only the very slightest embellishments permitted once in a while when he could find a momentary gap to fill. Then, sometime in the 1940s, the modern jazz pioneers—Charlie Parker, Dizzy Gillespie, Thelonius Monk—started giving their rhythm men solo space.

Most bassists, suddenly confronted with two or three minutes to fill with improvised music (and the audience actually listening to them!) probably dreamed of occupying the time with a tuneful solo, executed with the bow, like a cellist. Two things prevented them: first, the fact that they could not be spared from their rhythm function long enough even to pick up the bow; and, secondly, their inability to use a bow at all. (A third reason occurs to me: they didn't *own* a bow.)

So they plucked away, *pizzicato* as ever, trying to turn their unwieldy rhythm machines into fluent melodic instruments. They failed, of course, or most of them did. A few, notably Ray Brown, succeeded against all the odds, and created solos that were both interesting and reasonably exciting—though how often these solos would stand up to analysis if transcribed and played on a more conventional instrument is open to question.

The bassist having bumbled out his required two or three choruses, the drummer then expected to have his turn. He, of course, could not play anything resembling a tune. No one really wants to hear a single drum being struck intermittently, however ingenious the rhythms, so drum solos became simply a matter of building the intensity of the tattoo—the wildness of the showmanship—to a point where the audience felt it was seeing something astonishing, like a juggler with ten balls in the air or a dog walking on its hind legs. Only the very rarest of jazz drummers—Buddy Rich was among them—managed to retain a sense of musicality, almost of melodic invention, during those protracted solo drum passages.

While the bassist took his solo the structure of the music had continued by implication, since he, like the wind soloists, was working to the chord structure. But when the drummer started his farrago, the music no longer had any perceptible shape at all. Within a matter of seconds the tempo would rise or fall to one at which he could execute his most glittering tricks. Neither the performer nor his listeners troubled to keep his place in the structure of the chorus. In short, there was total creative freedom for the soloist.

As I suggested in my previous letter, when there are no rules the game is not worth playing, and at jazz concerts when the drummer takes his marathon solo you will notice that the rest of the musicians promptly leave the stage, ostensibly to leave the spotlight to him, but in fact to have a game of poker in the wings. They are summoned back in the end, grumbling, by a special code signal which is one of the truly international signposts of music:

During one such inordinately long and battering drum solo at a London theatre I came to a decision. No, it merited a capital letter: it was a Decision. I decided that I had had enough. I stood up and quietly left the place. Since that day I have never voluntarily suffered another spotlit drum solo feature, still less paid to listen to one.

I hope, for your sake and everyone else's, that your young friend Bix is one of those splendid drummers who relish ensemble work more than the spotlit tattoo; who have to be almost bullied into 'trading fours', as the expression has it, with the trumpeter or tenor sax player—in other words alternating solo four-bar phrases. There are few innocent joys so great as feeling oneself an integral part of a really swinging jazz rhythm section. The drummer is without doubt the lynchpin of the section, and can make or mar the whole thing.

Next time you go to one of his band sessions you might notice how conscious the others are of his support. The drummer is the one whom all the others are hearing, registering, sometimes competing against. The bassist and the pianist could work away all night long without drawing a grin of praise or an uplifted eyebrow of disapproval.

If Bix's exuberance should flag, or alternatively get the better of him for a moment, he will immediately receive the wind player's Seal of Disapproval: the bell of the instrument turned full in his face. That is his cue to tone it down, step it up, stop filling in so fussily, or perhaps to change from sticks to wire brushes.

The messages that jazz musicians manage to pass to one another without a word being spoken have long fascinated me. Their music being more tradition-bound than almost any other, there is less basically that requires to be said: working within a strict tempo, a single key and unvarying four-four time, communication is seldom necessary. However, it does take place, very often without the audience having much idea that anything is happening.

The average impromptu jazz session begins with a simple initial question: which tune to play? Even this much is sometimes left to a signal rather than to a verbal decision. The trumpeter may tootle the first three quick notes of *Perdido*. Taking his cue, the pianist, whose job it is to start the music going, will begin to improvise an introduction in the accepted *Perdido* key of B flat, weaving a fleeting hint of the melody into his note pattern as a general indication of which tune has been chosen. The choice of tempo is his, though *Perdido* has a kind of built-in tempo of its own which is unlikely to be varied by more than a fraction.

After a few seconds the drummer joins in, picking up the time and reinforcing the beat. But not the bassist, because the pianist is not yet working to any set harmonic pattern and their respective bass notes would clash. It is as if the pianist is saying, 'We're going to play *Perdido* in B flat. Get set, and wait.'

Wait for what? For the end of the pianist's four-bar introduction, when the rest of the players are expected to come in with their unison statement of the tune. But it may be that the trumpeter doesn't feel quite ready. So he turns away to brush his mouth with his wrist, or shakes the accumulated water from his instrument. (Not 'spit', by the way, just condensation from his breath.) This is the pianist's signal to extend his introduction by a further four bars.

Then—bang. In comes everybody, with the 32-bar theme of *Perdido*.

As this initial statement-chorus is ending, the leader inclines his trumpet bell towards the first man who is to take a solo, perhaps the tenor sax player. He, picking up his cue, carries the last unison phrase into a running figure of his own, asserting his claim to the solo space. He begins to play completely impromptu melodic phrases, based on the chords which the pianist and bassist are outlining in his support— F7 / F7 / B♭ / B♭ / F7 / F7 / B♭ / B♭—the familiar harmonic sequence runs through every player's consciousness, like a motorist driving along a familiar road.

Strictly speaking, there is no limit to the number of 32-bar choruses the tenor saxophonist may feel disposed to play. If things are going well, and the others are encouraging him, he may still be rhapsodizing away five or six choruses later. (On one celebrated occasion a Duke Ellington sax star played almost 40 successive choruses, while the crowd still howled for more.) But inspiration can suddenly fail; a lip can tire; the soloist may feel the sudden urge for a mouthful of beer or a drag on a cigarette, in which case during the last eight bars of one of the choruses he will angle his 'horn' (in jazz all wind instruments are 'horns') in the direction of another player, inviting him to take over.

A less obvious signal that ideas have run dry is to use an acknowledged cliché phrase in the torrent of otherwise original ideas. The cliché used may be a standing joke among musicians; for example anyone who inserted

64

in an otherwise respectable solo would clearly be trying to draw his colleagues' attention to *something*, even if it were only the arrival in the club of an agent who owed them money.

Every jazzman has his own personal collection of clichés, perhaps of his own invention, but clichés none the less. It has to be remembered that a jazz solo is not a totally spontaneous creation, rather is it a series of permutations based on the soloist's mental repertoire of phrases; a very large repertoire perhaps, but a personal collection of known phrases all the same. The order in which they come to the player's mind is triggered off by the promptings of key, chord and context.

Famous personal flags of this kind include Lester Young's

Charlie Parker's rather similar little phrase

John Dankworth's

and Oscar Peterson's finger-taxing repeated phrase

against a 4/4 time-signature. For all the excitement he generates, Peterson is the most cliché-ridden of all contemporary jazz masters, permutating his stock phrases with no apparent attempt to avoid them or (having involved himself in them) to evade their iron grip.

being one that I, as a listener, have come to dread. Not to mention

While the left hand fills any available two-beat gap with

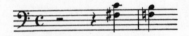

But to return to the jazz group as a whole: when all the soloists have had an extended turn, the leader may indicate, again without a word being spoken, that the time has come for an exchange of eight or four bar improvised phrases.

This he does simply by playing eight bars himself and turning sharply to the next soloist in line. Even the long-suffering bassist and drummer may be allotted some solo space under this arrangement. Then, finally, when the eights and fours have been exhausted, the last improvising player might introduce a hint of the *Perdido* melody into his melodic pattern, and the rest, taking the hint, will line up to play a final unison chorus.

The end? Not quite. However neat, tidy and well organized the quarter-hour of *Perdido*-based improvisation may have been, I can almost guarantee that the final chord will be a rambling mess.

This is because—I say it again—jazzmen are of all musicians the most conservative, the most tradition-bound. Once a convention grows up in jazz usage it is almost impossible to dislodge it. Thus for decade after decade every jazz number had what is known in the trade as a 'tramline ending'. It simply ran off the rails at the terminus—

‖ 1   2   3   4 ‖ 1   2   stop

At long last this convention became discredited and was superseded by the pause-ending, during which every player hangs on to the last note as long as he can, soaring up and down and trying to finish on a note as far removed as possible from the basic notes of the home chord.

An exceptionally irritating example of this practice can be heard at the end of nearly every item played by that otherwise impeccable pianist, Oscar Peterson. However brilliantly imagined and executed Peterson's performance, from the fastest romp to the slowest ballad, the final chord is always played *tremolando* and extended on and on and on. ('If only he won't do it just this once,' I beg the gods. But he does.)

Your drummer friend will know all about pause-endings, tramlines, eights and fours, not to mention the self-descriptive 'We want Charlie' intro. As a drummer he will have a language of his own consisting of paradiddles, daddy-mammys, flams and rim shots, hi-hats and chokes, while the mention of 'matched Zildjians' will bring either a smile to his face or a tear to his eye, depending on whether or not he owns such a brace of cymbals.

He will also know that in jazz argot 'to have a blow' means to join in a happy improvising session, whether or not one's instrument happens to be of the blown variety. He will also know, perhaps having found out the hard way, that when calling out the tempo at the start of a number it is unwise to count 'one—two—', since half the musicians will expect a 'three—four—' to follow and will fail to start, just to be on the safe side. So Bix, if he is the leader (and I expect any boy friend of yours to be!) will never actually utter the words 'one—

two—'. 'Three—four—' he will call, and the band will start playing on the next beat. No one in jazz ever called out 'Five—'. Perhaps that's what is wrong with it.

Your affectionate

Steve

13

My Dear Pat

I am delighted to learn that Bix is the leader of his band, and even more glad that he has some sympathy with my depressing experiences at the receiving end of *fortissimo* drum solos at jazz concerts. I am also intrigued to learn that he is experimenting with alternative endings to the tramline and the pause-chord. I wish him luck. As he rightly points out, the real cliché is neither the one nor the other, but *both*—

The best news of all, though, was in the very last paragraph of your letter. How splendid of you to summon up your courage and march up to Carl Birdcage at that party and tell him exactly what you thought of his *Monodic Lesions*—numbers I to IX! I'll bet that had him at VIs and VIIs. How I would love to have seen his face!

I must say his reply to you suggests a certain arrogance, not to mention a deplorably limited vocabulary. I am old-fashioned enough to think that young men ought not to speak to young ladies in that way, even at cocktail parties.

Just for curiosity I have been working out what our Mr Birdcage may have made financially out of his IXth *Monodic Lesion*. Putting together the Contemporary Music Council's grant, the donation from the Musica Futura Foundation, the grant in aid from the Committee for the Dismemberment of the Classical Symphonic Concept (CDCSC) and his royalties from the two broadcasts which you and I heard, it seems to me that he has something like £4,000 coming his way. No wonder he was wearing a 'lovely maroon velvet jacket' at the party. Not that I begrudge any composer his royalties.

There was once a French composer of light music and operetta, who went out to dine at a *Café-Concert* in Paris. As he sat there eating his way happily through the *carte*, the orchestra played music . . . *His* music.

Very gratifying, you might think. But when the bill arrived he refused to pay it. Sending for the manager, he observed that if his music was to be played in public without any payment he saw no reason why he should pay for his dinner; food for the soul being equivalent to food for the stomach.

The restaurant took him to court, and the amazing thing is that the composer won his case. The court agreed with him. That was in 1849 and it was one of the best things that has ever happened in the profession of music. Very French, too.

Just in case it should cross your mind to wonder *why* a composer deserves to be paid money when his compositions are played in public, may I remind you that music is, after all, *property*; intellectual property in a sense but, none the less, property. It may not be poached or illegally borrowed, any more than I may poach the trout in your stream or 'borrow' the deer from your game park. Even the cream off the top of your milk bottle is your property, and if I want it I must at least ask you and, if required to do so, make restitution. (Unless I am a blue-tit.)

To put it in four words, even composers must live. Poor fellows, they suffer from the same compulsion to feed their wives and children as do less favoured mortals. They too like to have a roof over their heads and a well-stocked cellar beneath their feet.

So it is that 'royalties', as they are called, are paid by broadcasting organizations and public halls whenever copyright music is performed. For a professional full-time composer it is often the only source of income he has. So spare a copper, and willingly, for the man who makes the music you enjoy, Pat.

Getting money from one's music is not quite the same as writing for money. We're told that Beethoven refused to finish reading Sir Walter Scott's *Kenilworth* because, he complained, 'This man writes for money.' It was a cutting remark, and Beethoven was hardly the one to cast the first stone when it came to being money conscious. What the composer of *Fidelio* presumably meant was that the great author had produced a pot-boiler. Scott's *Battle Symphony*, as you might say.

Birdcage did well out of those first two broadcast performances of his newly commissioned work. Not as well as someone in the teenage pop business, perhaps, but then he is not in the record-selling racket. To compensate for that, the royalty collecting society of which he is a member creates a deliberate (and very large) imbalance in the 'per minute' payments made to serious writers as opposed to those in the pop world. You would be surprised—and so would some of the pop writers—to know the extent of that loading in favour of 'serious' music.

But to your letter. You enclosed a manuscript song written by your friend Bix, and there is no point in denying the fact: I think it is an excellent piece of work. His musical literacy (and him a drummer, to boot!) is impeccable, and the tune has been on my mind ever since I first looked at it. Excellent.

And quite unpublishable. No one records nice old-fashioned songs like that any more and since no one records them, no one wants to publish them either. Song publishing was yesterday's game; today the activity is record merchandizing, and even that seems to be seriously on the wane. Bix's insistence on wanting to 'find a publisher' for his song betrays a somewhat naïve notion as to how the popular song industry is run these days.

The golden age of the 32-bar chorus is over, more's the pity. Rodgers, Hart, Hammerstein, Berlin, Kern, Porter, the Gershwin brothers . . . What marvels of conciseness they created! And how one still misses the thrill of hearing for the first time new songs like *All the Things you Are, Small Hotel* or *Embraceable You*. Only Stephen Sondheim writes songs like that any more, and even for him there seem to be no single songs, only Broadway musicals with their elaborate scores and complex international agreements. It is significant that Britain's brilliant young team of Tim Rice and Andrew Lloyd Webber do not write songs at all (though their operas may include them).

Nowadays it's pop, isn't it? Pop groups, single record hits; the instant failure, the instant fortune.

The first and most important point to be made about today's pop songs is that any fool can write one. It takes no great talent or training to knock up a hummable tune or to put together a few doggerel lines of quasi-verse. There is an amateur song-writer in every street—sometimes I suspect in every house—assiduously putting together the half page of musical and verbal platitudes which constitute the currency of Tin Pan Alley. 'The enclosed song is as good as anything in the Top Thirty,' they write in their covering letters. Exactly.

The difference between their trivial songs and the trivial songs being recorded and broadcast by the stars is that the latter were written by the recording artists themselves, their executives or their friends. That should come as no surprise: in a village where everyone grows roses, it is the squire's rose which wins at the flower show. By the same token if any half-intelligent person can knock out a pop song in thirty minutes, the people with patronage are not going to turn to the unknown amateur for their supply.

This simple, honest advice is naturally hard for the average songwriter to accept. Before his tune is even down on paper he is in love with it. To criticize his brain-child, much as he may implore you to do exactly that, is like telling a new parent that his baby will look better when it has some hair and a few teeth. Amateur songwriters do not want to be told the truth. They want to be told how to make a million pounds.

That being so, the way some of them go about it is truly remarkable. After all, they are playing for extremely high stakes. Yet they mail off tatty manuscripts, ill-recorded tapes and cassettes, enclosing covering letters which apologize for poor performance and even for uncompleted songs. They submit a great wad of manuscripts, as if to say, 'Here, *you* sort out this lot and see if one of them might be of some good. As far as I'm concerned they're all the same.' All masterpieces.

Financially such people are playing for the highest rewards, yet they seem unprepared to spend a few pounds on presenting their creations in the best light. The wise amateur song-writer—and I concede that there must be a few—realizes that if he wants to make fifty thousand pounds out of his brain-waves, it might be prudent to spend one per cent of that amount in getting a first-class demonstration tape made.

Once done, he will send it (but having first enquired if he may) to someone in the professional record-making business who may be prepared to devote two minutes of his time to placing the cassette in his playback machine and giving that instant opinion which his experience over the years has made so valuable.

Such a person will simply not be prepared to spool through false starts or suffer a recording made on the cheap using some-body's front room piano. He will not be the least bit interested in a song written in the style of the 1930s, submitted in the hope that 'surely true melody is due for a revival any day now'. He is a businessman operating in the toughest of business worlds and nothing in his contract says that he should spend even one minute of his time doing charitable work among deluded amateurs.

I am aware that these are strong sentiments. I should make it clear that I do not regard myself as being that experienced someone in the record business referred to above. I merely know that such people exist: it is the ambitious songwriter's business to discover for himself who such people are and where they are to be found.

Of course, *some* songwriting hopefuls must be successful, otherwise there would ultimately be no successful profes-sionals. Strictly speaking, it isn't impossible to break in, only *nearly* impossible. The popular music industry is tough, though, and virtually impregnable. With billions lying around inside, Fort Knox has to have high walls.

A very few songwriters do break down the barriers and they themselves are the tough ones. Music publishers tell heart-rending stories of shameless songwriters who collect advance royalty cheques by peddling the same song to rival firms, or who plead artistic forgetfulness while signing exclusive contracts with two competing publishers. The writers have their cautionary tales, too. But a conscientious publisher, having acquired a new work from the composer in exchange for half his potential income, will set out to exploit the piece and publicize it. He will make sure that it is heard by record company and film executives. In short, the composer having done his bit, it is now up to the music publisher to do his.

The less efficient, less principled publisher will do nothing whatever, content to grab half of what little may dribble in from the copyright which he now owns jointly with the composer. There are a few such publishers still around; enough to worry their more reputable brethren and to keep the wise composer alert to the need for careful choice when it comes to signing with a publishing firm.

But things change. In the much altered pop scene of today the songwriter is likely to be his own publisher, even the majority shareholder in his own record producing company.

There are specific occasions when it is simply not a good idea to have one's work published at all. If a piece of music is already guaranteed plenty of major performances—a television signature tune perhaps, or an advertising 'jingle'—it would be madness voluntarily to sign away half one's proceeds by letting a publisher in on the deal, since there may be nothing he can do to increase its earnings. I was responsible for many hundreds of TV jingles, but I am happy to say that not one of them was ever shared with a publisher. I am a generous chap, but philanthropic work among music publishers is something I leave to others. And now, of course, any holes there may have been in the signature tune and jingle dike have been plugged up by nominal publishing firms set up by the commissioning bodies.

When young Bix writes to me in his covering note that he seeks a publisher for his song, what he really seeks is a record company executive, who in turn will lean on a recording artist, who will find a way to catch the public's ear. Believe me, the music publishers will then form a queue for the pleasure of taking Bix out to lunch at any restaurant he cares to name between Rome and Rio de Janeiro.

Till then, I don't honestly know what to suggest he should do. Maybe get out his drum kit and play a long loud solo . . . It might make him forget about wanting to be a popular song-writer.

Dear, dear Pat—I cannot get over what Carl Birdcage said to you, the insolent puppy. I'll bet you quelled him with *one look*!

You are my favourite girl. And *I* am your affectionate friend

Steve

14

Dear Pat

Bix took my criticisms and comments very coolly and I am grateful to you for passing on his thanks. My thanks to him, too, for his interesting thoughts on what makes a great song.

Yes, I do agree: it's the moment of magic. Most songs, even the better ones, are conventional enough. Then suddenly there is an unexpected note or chord; a twist in the harmony; a word in the lyric that catches the imagination, as the word 'huckleberry' does in Johnny Mercer's *Moon River*.

Thinking through some of the old standard evergreen songs of the Thirties and Forties it is noticeable that while some of them had sheer quality throughout, many more had that sudden flash, a moment of 'rightness' that carried an otherwise fairly pedestrian song into a new life of immortality. Harold Arlen's *Get Happy*: what could be more prosaic than its main phrase? And what more ear-catching than the descending phrase that begins at the words 'We're heading 'cross the river . . .'? The old jazz standard, *Idaho*, is as dull as ditchwater for 24 of its 32 bars, but the middle eight bars are ingenious and original.

Even Jerome Kern's *The Song is You* has no great appeal until he begins that strangely searching middle strain, then excels

76

himself in the last phrase with a surprise note on the words 'sing' and 'spring'.

Did I refer to the 'middle eight' of *Idaho*? It isn't, of course: it's the third of four eight-bar phrases, as the 'middle eight' usually is. It is the middle only in the sense that one has heard the first strain twice and is ready for something new, before the last strain rounds things off. So we have the standard chorus form of A A B A, as in *Oh! Lady be Good* or *If I Loved You*. No doubt the best word for the middle bit is the one used in America: the *bridge*.

Both those standard songs are by now so familiar that we can no longer hope to hear them with an innocent ear. Both had their moments of magic though. In the case of *Oh! Lady be Good*—let's have the name right: only the show was called *Lady be Good!*—it was the chord on the second bar at the word 'lovely' that brought a harmonic pang to an otherwise rather bland melody line.

In Richard Rodgers's *If I Loved You* the listener has to wait until the fourth bar of the bridge for a heart-tugging chord on the word 'shy'. It's things like that which make a song.

It goes without saying that the master composers of the classical era knew all about the magic moment and the reward that comes from finding the absolutely right note or chord. Beethoven's notebooks are crammed with examples of tunes which anyone else would have been glad to own but which he continually shaped, altered and rejected, until at last the perfect form was reached.

The scholarly but pleasingly playful musical lexicographer, Percy Scholes, once pointed out that the tremendous motif of the Fifth Symphony, said to denote 'fate knocking at the door'—

—would have been dreadfully weakened if Beethoven had settled for the perfectly acceptable but uninspired

77

To which I feel tempted to add that he might even have been prepared to settle for a kind of warbling cuckoo-call—

That would really have cooked the Fifth Symphony's goose!

More than most, Beethoven was prepared to change his mind if he felt it necessary. His friend and pupil, Czerny, reported that some time after the first performance of the Choral Symphony Beethoven told a group of friends that he now realized what a mistake the final movement had been and wanted to withdraw the score from performance, replacing it with a purely instrumental movement without any voices. 'In fact he already had an idea for it in his mind,' added Czerny.

That idea never came to light. What one wouldn't give to know what it was! But at least that episode gives posterity a slightly less scornful attitude to one Josef Rosenbaum, a member of the audience at the symphony's première, who jotted down in his notebook the crisp summary 'lovely, but tedious'. Beethoven, as we know, was inclined to agree. He would even have gone along with Spohr, who wrote: 'The first three movements of the Ninth Symphony, in spite of some isolated flashes of genius, are to my mind inferior to all the eight previous symphonies, while the fourth movement of that work is in my opinion so monstrous and tasteless that I can never bring myself to understand how a genius like Beethoven could have written it.'

The composer knows best? Yes, if he lives long enough to put his second thoughts into practice.

To return to the evergreen songs of the Gershwin/Kern/

Rodgers/Porter/Berlin era, the thing that makes those great songwriters so extraordinary is the very narrow range within which they worked. Imagine saying what you have to say within a virtually inflexible 32 bars! Even the supreme miniaturist Franz Schubert gave himself more elbow room than that.

The limitations were, of course, self imposed. But a few of the master songwriters were at pains to disguise the restrictions of the form they had accepted. The British team of Eric Maschwitz and Jack Strachey broke the obligatory bridge rule in 1935 with a *four*-bar bridge for *These Foolish Things*. All was well at first. Then their American publishers started counting the bars and told them to go back to the drawing-board and come up with a bridge of the proper length. To this day the British public knows a middle *four* bars of that song which is quite different from the American-accepted middle *eight*— though the words are the same for both.

Then there were the Gershwins. Having completed their song, *I'm Bidin' my Time*, in the customary A A B A 32-bar chorus form, they had sufficient detachment to see that the chorus felt long and a little tedious. So they cut out the second strain altogether, creating the very rare form (in Tin Pan Alley terms) of A B A. Other songwriters ought sometimes to have copied their example.

One of the most striking of magic moments in the classic popular song repertoire comes as the result of a surprise note that would have surprised the composer! The lovely song, *Moonlight in Vermont*, starts with the words 'Pennies in a stream; falling leaves, a sycamore', with a tenderly appealing un-expected note on the syllable 'more'.

But the note (C flat in the key of E flat) does not appear anywhere in the printed and published copy: it is a plain and much less interesting B flat. Who was the singer, or conceivably the inventive rehearsal pianist, whom the composer has reason to thank? Incidentally, that same song is unusual in yet another respect, since in the whole of the chorus lyric there is not one single rhyme. And to mark still further the unusual nature of the song, it consists of three strains of six bars and one

79

of eight, totalling 26 bars in all. Taken all round, *Moonlight in Vermont* is a strange creation . . . and as beautiful as the state it honours.

Another curiosity for your friend Bix's archive. The original 1929 song copy of Nacio Herb Brown's *Singin' in the Rain* surprisingly shows that it was the composer who thought up the famous Gene Kelly introductory phrase beginning

rather than Kelly himself, or his arranger for the 1952 film who has so often been credited with a brainwave.

Another oddity—I'm warming up now!—is Nat Cole's hit, *Unforgettable*, a simple and not-particularly-remarkable 32-bar song, but which starts in one key (G) and ends in another (C), thus making repeated choruses difficult without a modulation. The same may in a sense be said of *Come Rain or Come Shine*, which ends up in the key of its submediant.

A much underrated song that starts in the major but goes into the tonic minor key (and incidentally finds its way back again brilliantly) is Milton Ager's *A Bench in the Park*. It predates Cole Porter's *I Love Paris* by a good many years, another song which enjoys a major/minor pivot, but goes much more conventionally between the two. It ends up sounding as though it wants to slip back into the minor again, not having established the major tonality, at least not to this listener's satisfaction. It is one of the very few Cole Porter tunes that peter out, for all the world as though the composer had lost interest. Even the words of that last line are depressingly conventional for so unconventional a songwriter. ,

Singers naturally revel in a song that gives them the chance of a big dramatic finish, with outspread arms, head thrown back and a *fortissimo* last note that brings the audience to its feet. *My Way* is the leader in that field: a singer's song if ever there was one. Indeed it was written by a singer, Paul Anka. Not to his taste, I imagine, would be the old Doris Day song *It's*

Magic, surely unique among standard songs in having a first note which is the highest note of the whole song, leaving the singer with nothing to throw at the audience by way of a climax.

Not that the highest note in a song need be the very last one, as Rodgers and Hammerstein proved with *You'll Never Walk Alone*, chanted *falsetto* by football crowds who lack the forethought to start in a low key.

Effective though a high note can be, such things are not welcomed by singers in the early part of a song. A cautionary example is Victor Herbert's *Sweethearts*, which extends the performer within its first eight bars but offers him nothing later on to draw the applause. Its melody covers a massive range of two octaves all but a note; an unusual span for a song that peters out at the end.

The record? That goes to a popular ballad of rather later date, Frank Sinatra's *Over and Over*. Its second strain begins with just five beats that cover a full two octaves! Sinatra seldom chooses the song for his concert appearances nowadays, I notice. And who shall blame him?

As for *White Christmas* . . . But perhaps that had better wait for another letter.

Your affectionate

Steve

15

Dear Pat

Where was I? Oh yes, *White Christmas*. Did you know what happened when Irving Berlin sat at the piano and played over that song for the first time to Bing Crosby?

'. . . And may all your Christmases be white,' he sang. There was a long silence.

Then the phlegmatic Bing drew his pipe out of his mouth. 'Irving,' he said, in one of the most massive understatements of Tin Pan Alley history, 'that's one you don't have to worry about.'

He was right.

'Usually,' Irving Berlin commented, 'Crosby never says anything.' Eight years later, fifty million records of the song had been sold in North America alone; when the overseas sale reports came in, they stopped counting. The sentiment is universal, the tune haunting. What more could anybody want? A last line that doesn't go down, perhaps, and many singers rewrite the final four notes to make them rise. The song has a range of a tenth (B to D) so that a singer whose comfortable vocal range was from A to E would be quite happy with it in the original key.

All popular singers know their ranges; rather less can tell

their accompanists the key in which they sing a given song. With most tunes this hardly matters, because the range they demand is relatively narrow. Yet heaven protect any vocalist who attempts *Old Man River*, with its range of a 14th, without first making sure the key is right!

Will you Remember?, the Jeanette Macdonald and Nelson Eddy song that begins 'Sweetheart, sweetheart, sweetheart . . .', is what singers would call 'rangy'. It starts comfortably and reassuringly in the centre of the singer's range, throws an unexpectedly low note at him, then lifts him to a high one in the very next line . . . and with worse to come.

'Ye gods, it goes up and down like a yo-yo!' a vocalist exclaimed to me once, before banishing it from his repertoire. The fact is that its *tessitura* is deceiving. What seems in prospect to be a low song turns out in the end to be a high one.

The *tessitura* is the 'lie' of a song, that part of the range where most of the notes occur. Think your way through *Climb Every Mountain* and you will notice that it has an unusually low *tessitura* until the last phrase. The song's range is not particularly wide as big production numbers go, but the last phrase feels like a scream to the singer who has mumbled his way through the earlier phrases. Performers find out from experience that in choosing a key for *Climb Every Mountain* it is all too easy to start too high, and almost impossible to start too low.

Ranges can be very deceptive. The Rodgers and Hart song, *Lover*, gives the impression of having a wide ranging tune, but in fact its main phrase is all contained within a mere four notes of the scale. (Only the bridge pushes it up an extra third.)

Though as a song it hardly deserves to be mentioned alongside such evergreen masterpieces, *When the Saints go Marching In* gets a mention in this context because it only uses five notes, like a piano student's five-finger exercise.

Vocally speaking, it is much easier to move by step— between adjacent notes of the scale—than in big jumps. Indulgent listener though I am, I have yet to hear anyone sing perfectly in tune a Benny Goodman jazz standard called *Don't be that Way*, in which these notes are called for rapidly

in the second bar. Pitch those accurately at speed, and you are ready to take on Schoenberg's *Pierrot Lunaire*!

A singer wanting to get familiar with the notes of the pentatonic scale—though I can't think why—could do no better than sing Maurice Chevalier's *Louise*, which apart from its bridge is pentatonic from start to finish. An older and lesser known song of 1914, *By the Waters of Minnetonka*, is pentatonic through the whole of its length except for a single bar at the end of the bridge, where presumably the composer lost his concentration for a moment.

Strange things indeed can happen in the bridges of songs. There are many cases of composers writing reasonably conventional A phrases, only to run the gamut of the keys in the B strain. Thus *Body and Soul* starts out on its lovely course for 16 diatonic bars. Then the composer slides up into an utterly remote key . . . then another . . . and finally, to be truthful, it is only by the skin of his teeth that he gets back to the home key in time for the last strain. The less highly rated *How High the Moon* wheels deliciously from key to key, but in this case the composer always knows how he is to get back.

Jerome Kern's *All the Things you are* has no sooner established its key than it is off on a countrywide tour, arriving at the half way mark while still several miles from home. Thanks to what has to be admitted is a bit of a cheat (known technically as an enharmonic change) Kern is able to set off again from the original point. But this time his courage fails him and there are no more harmonic shocks in store. As with all these old masterpieces, Kern's tune is so familiar now that we can hardly expect to hear it with fresh ears, but *All the Things you are* always faintly disappoints me when the journeyings of its first half are done, and the rest of the song stays safely in port.

I'm getting terribly hungry! Am I boring you?

While munching my raw carrot and water biscuit (penance for being nasty about Bix's songwriting chances) I fell to musing about evergreen songs that wander from their original key but find their way back convincingly, and I think the winner in that contest might well be Rodgers's *Have you Met Miss Jones?* As in *Body and Soul* the first half is all 'on the white notes', so to speak. But then comes the bridge, and away go the harmonies on a wild excursion, getting back by the skin of their teeth in time for the white note last strain. Exactly the same analysis could be applied to Kern's *I Won't Dance*.

Many musician friends of my acquaintance would put forward *Laura* as being the most harmonically interesting of all the evergreen standard songs. Certainly its lyric, by the incomparable Johnny Mercer, is one of the relatively few popular songs that merit the word 'lyric' in the sense of being genuine lyric poetry. The music, by Dave Raksin, is certainly haunting. But the tune grows tortuous towards the end, and its final cadence—at least for this listener—is not convincing. Like *Unforgettable*, it ends up in the 'wrong' key.

It would be a mistake to think that all popular songs fall into the A A B A form. Many don't, for example *Our Love is Here to Stay*, which falls into two halves. Or *Tea for Two*, which has an unusual shape: an A phrase, followed by the same tune in a different key, then A again, and an entirely new melodic idea in the closing phrase.

A great song which uses no repetitive material at all is Kern's *They didn't Believe Me* (1914), which can only be summarized as A B C D, though towards the end Kern brings back the title figure from 'they didn't believe me' subtly altered to 'they'll *never* believe me'. You think I show signs of being obsessed with Kern? I admit it—the man was a marvel.

He was also a remarkably honest man, as the history of *The Last Time I saw Paris* testifies. After Paris fell to the Nazis in 1940 Oscar Hammerstein wrote his lyric about the city and Kern was invited to contribute the music. It was the only time that he wrote music *after* the words; in every other case his melody came first. It was the way he worked.

In due course Kern's and Hammerstein's song was nominated for an Academy Award, an Oscar. But Kern objected to the choice. He said, with commendable fairness, that since it had not been written expressly for a film the song was not strictly eligible. Instead he wanted the Oscar to go to Harold Arlen and Johnny Mercer for *That Old Black Magic*, a genuinely commissioned film song. Feeling strongly about it, Kern set out to use his influence in getting the Oscar rules changed so that in future only legitimate film songs could qualify.

These old songs are endlessly fascinating . . . at any rate to me. I am glad your friend Bix is not so jazz-obsessed that he cannot enjoy the works of these master composers of the twentieth century. I know from your last letter that he gets fun out of analysing them, as I do.

Here's a test for him: a few teasers based on standard songs of 1920–60. Ask him:

1) Which Gershwin tune is 34 bars long, thanks to an interrupted cadence?

2) Which Vincent Youmans song (apart from its bridge) uses only three notes?

3) Which much recorded song of 1960 has a lyric that ends with the same word repeated ten times? A word which, used three times, *begins* a Lionel Monckton success of 1910?

4) Which Gershwin song of 1937 has the same title as a Rodgers and Hammerstein song of 1951?

5) Which 1925 show by the Gershwins had the same title as a hit musical of 1956, and what was the title of the latter show when it was first announced in 1955?

6) Can you think of two song titles that begin with the word 'And', and two that begin with 'But'?

7) An enormously popular sentimental ballad, first published in Britain in 1936, consists of irregular bars, having beats of 4 3 4 4 3 3 4 2 and 3! What is it called?

And, finally,

8) Which jazz standard is this?

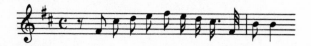

Let me know how the lad gets on, and give him my regards . . . Which is more than I ever said about Orpheus M. Pobjoy, come to think of it.

Your affectionate

Steve

16

My Dear Pat

Bix did well with the questions at the end of my last letter,
getting five out of the eight questions right. It was a particularly
good score for someone who wasn't even born when most of the
songs were written.

Just to check through the answers—

1) The 34-bar Gershwin tune is *I Got Rhythm*, with its
tacked-on repeat of the line 'Who could ask for anything
more?' triggered off by an interrupted cadence—in other
words a twist in the musical path that leads suddenly
uphill instead of down. Incidentally, Ira Gershwin used
exactly the same line at the end of the bridge in *Nice Work
if You can Get It*.

2) The three-note Vincent Youmans song is *Great Day*.
Only its bridge extends the number of notes to 11 in all.

3) The 1960 song, *Try to Remember*, ended with the word
'follow' sung ten times. Lionel Monckton's *The Pipes of
Pan* began 'Come follow, follow, follow . . .'

4) The Gershwin brothers wrote *Shall we Dance?* for Fred
Astaire and Ginger Rogers in 1937. Fourteen years later
Rodgers and Hammerstein wrote their *Shall we Dance?*
for Gertrude Lawrence and Yul Brynner. There is no
copyright in a title.

5) When the Gershwins took their 1920s show *Tell me More* on its try out tour they called it *My Fair Lady*. Thirty years later Lerner and Loewe announced their adaptation of Shaw's *Pygmalion* under the provisional title of *My Lady Liza*. The following year (1956) it was changed to *My Fair Lady*. The words come, of course, from the eighteenth-century nursery rhyme *London Bridge is Falling Down*. Yet 'my fair' is how Liza Doolittle would pronounce fashionable *Mayfair*, isn't it?

6) There must be many songs starting with the words 'And' or 'But'. Among them are *And the Angels Sing, And her Mother came Too, And the Great Big Saw came Nearer and Nearer, But Beautiful* and *But I Do (You Know I Do)*.

7) The ballad song with the extraordinary structure of irregular bars is Alan Murray's *I'll Walk Beside You*, with its alternating bars of 4/4, 3/4 and even 2/4. It is testimony to the innate rightness of the melody that the public at large did not reject so complicated a song but on the contrary took *I'll Walk Beside You* to its heart.

8) Which jazz standard? I rather hoped Bix wouldn't recognize it and he didn't! Let me explain.

The phrase of music I wrote down—

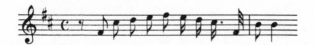

—was the subject of an astonishing court case at the beginning of the Twenties when Puccini, composer of *Tosca*, sued everyone concerned in the American popular song, *Avalon*. He claimed that the tune of *Avalon* had been stolen from his aria *E Lucevan le Stelle*, of which the most telling (though not the opening) phrase is the bar and a half quoted above.

The writers of *Avalon* were nominally Messrs Rose, Jolson and DeSylva. I say 'nominally' because no one will ever be quite sure to what extent Al Jolson genuinely contributed to the song copies on which his name appeared as joint-author, as opposed to merely justifying his share in the royalties by making the song popular. Plenty of famous performers have done the same and are still doing so. In fact, it isn't a bad bargain for the hopeful songwriter, who at least knows that he has one successful show business personality working on his song.

Puccini's legal action against Al Jolson and his associates duly came to court. As usual on such occasions the legal profession enjoyed itself hugely. 'Who cares if a fortune is about to change hands? We can have music in court!' At one point during the trial an instrumental trio was set up in the courtroom, with instructions to play the opening line of *Avalon* at the same time as a somewhat primitive phonograph record was churning out the contentious bar and a half from *Tosca*. Proof, one might say, if proof be needed. And needed it certainly was.

If the players were really clever and attentive I suppose they *could* have made the two pieces of music sound sufficiently alike for a learned judge to spot the similarity, but there must have been some appalling major/minor clashes, and I doubt if *Avalon* has ever before or since been played in the obscure key of B major.

I have never ceased to marvel that Judge Someone-or-other did not send Puccini and his lawyers packing, with a stern warning not to waste everybody's time in future but to see instead if he couldn't get a bit further with *Turandot*.

The differences between the two themes really are stronger than the similarities, the parallel passage in *Tosca* being less than five seconds long and set in the minor as opposed to the major. Even the note values are markedly different—though it has to be conceded that for ten notes the tunes do run rather alike. The court duly found in Puccini's favour, awarding him damages of $25,000, plus not merely a share in the proceeds but *all* the future royalties accruing from the song.

And that is how Puccini became the composer of *Avalon* and Al Jolson lost interest in plugging a number that bore his name. I don't suppose it mattered much a quarter of a century later, when Jolson's record of *Avalon* became one of four million-selling discs thanks to the Jolson biographical films.

There is an old music publishers' saying that goes 'After the hit comes the writ'. It is only too true that when a song has been internationally successful there is usually a writ to be expected from someone who claims to have 'composed' it first. In a field so commonplace as popular music it is hardly surprising if two people should happen on the same melodic notion. One might as well try to copyright a blade of grass.

So it was that in 1963 their Lordships Willmer, Upjohn and Diplock were called upon to decide whether a new and profitable song called *Why* had infringed an old and profitable song called *In a Little Spanish Town*.

As usual, both plaintiffs and defendants brought into court their expert witnesses: singers and instrumentalists whose brief was to demonstrate how extraordinarily alike the tunes were—or were not—as the case may be. (It is always important for each performer to know exactly which side he is supposed to be on before making his demonstration.)

To make comparison between the songs a little more difficult, *Spanish Town* was in four-time, while *Why* was in three. Nevertheless Mr Justice Willmer said in his judgement, 'I was readily able to recognize the tune of *Why* as a familiar one which I had heard on frequent previous occasions.' But then he went on to quote an earlier case. 'Infringement of copyright in music is not a question of note for note comparison, but falls to be determined by the ear as well as the eye,' he pointed out. And Mr Justice Diplock concurred, saying, 'Infringement of copyright is not a question of note for note comparison, but of whether the *substance* is taken or not.'

The court had a splendid time discussing the question of what had been called 'unconscious copying', an expression which one side claimed (rightly, one would have thought) to be a contradiction in terms. If you are copying something, they maintained, it *must* be a conscious act, otherwise you are not copying at all, merely suffering from the long arm of coincidence. Take your choice between bad intention or bad luck, but don't coin a solecism like 'unconscious copying'.

Much of the case rested on whether or not the composer of

Why, who was a young American musician, might reasonably be thought to have heard, perhaps even played, the old jazz standard *In a Little Spanish Town*. He claimed that he hadn't, though claiming that you *don't* remember something is a little less convincing than claiming that you *do*. On this point Mr Justice Upjohn commented, 'I think it possible that Mr De Angelis *did* hear it and possibly played it in his early youth.' Certainly, it had been heard a great deal: at the time of the case there were 82 different recorded versions in the BBC Record Library.

In favour of the young American was the fact that even *In a Little Spanish Town* did not appear to be entirely original. It had much in common with an old song called *Let us Sing Merrily* and even with an Austrian folk tune from the previous century. This was crucial. It is a state of affairs devoutly hoped for, indeed prayed for every night, by the defendants in such cases: to find a non-copyright work which pre-dates both compositions and, therefore, from which both might be said to have been copied. Seeking out such early works can be quite a profitable sideline for musical researchers.

To put the *Spanish Town v. Why* case in non-legal terms: who stole what from whom and, if so, when? And anyway was it deliberate?

Three of Her Majesty's most learned Judges of Appeal duly gave their unanimous opinion. They dismissed the appeal. In other words they decided that when Peter De Angelis composed *Why* he had not consciously copied *In a Little Spanish Town*.

And here is one musician who thinks they were absolutely right. That sequential tune could have occurred to anyone working in the popular song market.

It was another legal luminary, Mr Justice Cross, who presided over the 1960 hearing that involved the much loved singer, Vera Lynn, and a song of hers—or *was* it hers?—called *Travelling Home*.

When Vera's record of *Travelling Home* reached the ears of a certain Scottish family they blew their top, and Scots tops blow fiercely, as we Sassenachs know. The family of the late Sir

Hugh Roberton, eminent founder of the Glasgow Orpheus Choir and arranger of much of its repertoire, felt strongly that *Travelling Home* was too much of a coincidence in view of Sir Hugh's well known *Westering Home*. Most musicians, if asked, would have said that *Westering Home* was traditional, in public domain, and totally free of copyright restrictions. They might have overlooked the fact that an arrangement, even of a traditional song, carries its own copyright protection.

The coincidence suggested by the titles, not to mention the music, did seem rather striking. Vera Lynn's record was very properly withdrawn from sale for the moment, and everyone moved into court to determine the matter.

The case lasted four days. Once again the legal profession enjoyed a musical interlude. A piano was pushed into court for demonstration purposes; Scottish pipers gave practical evidence that they knew the tune under a variety of names ranging from *Isle of my Heart* to *The Mucking of Geordie's Byre*. ('Would the witness repeat that last title?' requested the learned judge, pen in hand.)

Sir Hugh Roberton's contribution to *Westering Home* had indeed been to arrange it rather than to compose it. But the courtroom heard what most music businessmen already knew: that the arranger may stand in the place of the composer if the latter is no longer known. The score he creates, if identifiably his, enjoys the law's protection in full, even if the royalties he receives are less than he would get for an original composition.

Arranging, Mr Justice Cross reminded his hearers, did not necessarily mean composing. 'It is possible,' he said, 'that Sir Hugh independently hit upon the same eight bars as those older Scots tunes.' This was too much for one musical expert who maintained that such a thing would have been incredible.

In the end the judge held that the plaintiffs—Lady Helen Roberton, her two sons and the publishers concerned—had not made out their case. There was, therefore, no infringement.

This rather startling judgement allowed the Vera Lynn record to resume its sale, but it never quite recovered from the period of suspension while the hearing had been taking place. Vera had lost a hit through the Roberton family's intervention, or so she and her husband claim to this day. But a rather pleasing postscript came in 1975. Sir Hugh Roberton's contribution to musical pleasure having been so justly honoured by a knighthood, precisely the same recognition came to the defendant when, at the Queen's hand, Vera Lynn, singer, became Dame Vera Lynn DBE. Perhaps we may claim that the story had a happy ending after all. Certainly the Roberton estate continued to prosper from its copyrights. I don't think Vera Lynn recorded another Scottish folk tune.

The aphorism 'After the hit comes the writ' must have been on the lips of the music publisher involved when George Harrison's *My Sweet Lord* hit the heights of the pop charts in 1971 and the copyright owners of a song called *He's so Fine*, recorded by a group called the Chiffons, sued for infringement.

According to a press report, an American judge, claiming to have spent 'hours listening to the two songs'—really? *hours?*—gave his opinion that 'it is perfectly obvious in musical terms the two songs are identical'. Nevertheless, he went on to clear George Harrison of intentional copying, discoursing learnedly at some length about the Harrison subconscious and other metaphysical concepts which are not usually the subject of discussion on the side streets off Broadway.

Over at the London end it was Mr Justice Slade who gave judgement in the matter, demonstrating how on-the-ball he was by slipping into his summing-up the title of a current Cliff Richard hit. (The reference went down rather well in court.) The upshot of the hearing was that a commercial settlement was reached 'on mutually acceptable terms'. For once it may have been members of the musical profession who profited from the action instead of the members of the legal profession.

Who got what, as a result of that settlement, is not known—at least not by me. I do know that everyone involved successfully in the creation of popular music has to be on his guard against assuming that his new brainchild has not already been fathered by some other fortunate composer. The lesson is clear: never assume that what you have just written is new. Indeed my advice to all composers is that their first act on completing a new work should be to play the piece over to their wives with

94

the request, 'Tell me, darling, what does this remind you of?'

To be the victim of inadvertent plagiarism is one thing; to suffer as a result of doing insufficient research is quite another. Songwriters, like obedient children, should always do their homework. Songs written by composers who have been dead for 50 years or more are generally speaking freely available for use or, to put it more plainly, for theft. But even here there can be pitfalls. As I have already suggested, although the tune may be out of copyright the treatment or edition may not be. Furthermore, songwriters have a nasty trick of not having died quite so long ago as one imagines. I confess that I was once caught that way by the late lamented (though later lamented than I thought) Rimsky-Korsakov.

Those responsible for *Happy Birthday to You* did rather well out of writs and infringement actions, the lady who wrote the tune surviving until the year 1916 and the lyricist until 1946. Just in case, Pat, any prospective musical pirate of your acquaintance should be adding together 1946 and 50 in order to work out the year in which he can successfully hijack *Happy Birthday to You*, I might add that there was a copyright renewal in 1963.

So tell Bix to leave it alone. He would do better to write a new birthday song, to the tune of *Avalon*. But warn him to have his royalties paid in *lire*, just in case.

Your affectionate

Steve

17

My Dear Pat

Well! That Carl Birdcage should actually stop you in the street like that and lecture you on your failure to appreciate his music! You don't actually say so, but I'm sure you gave him a piece of your mind. Arrogant folk like Birdcage should be kept off the streets while honest hard-working citizens like Pat Ford are about their lawful purposes.

How is Bix? You didn't mention him in your last letter, though I assume it was he who took you to the Promenade Concert at the Royal Albert Hall.

('Why do you call it *the* Royal Albert Hall?' asked an American friend of mine. 'Do you say *the* Carnegie Hall, *the* Wembley Stadium, *the* Burlington House?' No, but we say *the* Royal Academy and *the* Festival Hall, don't we, Pat?)

I am glad you were so overcome by Brahms' First Symphony on hearing it last week. 'It will be long and not particularly amiable,' Brahms told a friend. He was right. But who would require that great music should be amiable?

One of the marvels about that symphony is the way it starts. One moment the listener is in a state of expectant silence . . . Then suddenly the great intellectual argument begins. We are hurled into the centre of a writhing coil of music that toils

96

upwards towards some seemingly unattainable goal. What an opening!

Getting going—making an immediate start—is not a thing that all composers find easy to pull off. Sir Arthur Bliss used to tell a delightful story about how as a youngster he took some inflated score of his to be looked at by Gustav Holst. All young composers write long pieces, and this was longer than most.

The older man looked at the first page, reading it to himself... Turned over... Scanned the next page... the next... and so on, until after several pages of silently reading young Bliss's music, he looked up and said encouragingly, 'Excellent, excellent! But when is it going to *begin*?'

Bliss told me that he never forgot that advice.

Brahms' First Symphony *begins*, immediately and challengingly. This is magnificent music, wonderfully argued. And when that engrossing opening movement came to its end at your Promenade Concert I'm not surprised that one or two people started to applaud.

Not you, Pat, of course. I realize that you would always bow to the conventions of concertgoing and save your handclapping for the permitted place after the last movement is ended and the conductor has signalled applause by dropping his arms and smiling at the players. But has it ever occurred to you to wonder *why* we are not allowed to clap as the first movement of a symphonic work reaches its end?

The pundits will tell you that the reason for the convention is because the composer has a full-scale plan, a carefully spaced argument which he wants to put across to the listener without interruption. Part of this master plan concerns the key relationships between the various movements, and if we were to take advantage of an interim pause for a burst of happy applause we might lose our key-sense. There is certainly a deliberate key relationship in the Brahms First Symphony, each movement beginning a major third higher than its predecessor: a neat touch, which it would be a shame to miss.

Why then have breaks between movements at all? Why separate them? Why do so many classical and romantic composers write endings to their first movements which almost compel an outbreak of applause?

Total silence between movements is a relatively recent thing. Even *during* movements the great masters were not necessarily averse to a bit of audible encouragement. Mendelssohn, writing to a friend, explained that in one of his concertos he had followed the cadenza with a loud orchestral passage 'because of course people will applaud the cadenza' and a quiet bit would, therefore, be lost. Tempering the wind to the shorn lamb? . . . or welcoming a bit of audience participation?

At the first performance of Beethoven's Choral Symphony the audience burst into spontaneous delighted applause near the start of the *scherzo* movement on hearing the solo *rat-a-tat* of the timpani in the fifth bar, while in the opera house, arias, duets and set-pieces are instantly applauded by any member of the audience who feels like it; this, although an opera—like a symphony or a concerto—is presumably part of a full-scale plan by the composer and should be listened to uninterrupted. Beethoven, presumably, applauded.

The rapt silence which is supposed to prevail between movements of the Beethoven Violin Concerto never fails to remind me of the very first performance, at which the soloist interspersed Beethoven's work with a few little novelty offerings of his own, during one of which he played with the violin upside down.

No one would want that sort of nonsense to be revived at a concert. But I confess to a slight feeling of regret that concerto first movements, especially those with *sforzando* endings, like Grieg's for piano or Sibelius' for violin, cannot be accorded an immediate storm of clapping by an audience dumbfounded with admiration at the sight of the soloist's flailing arms. Indeed, I find it hard to believe that the composers didn't deliberately invite it; certainly the soloists often do.

Where I would object to applause is in the very stillness between reflective movements of, say, a string quartet. To make any sound at all before the *lento* movement of Beethoven's op. 135 would be utterly insensitive. Any interruption there would be unthinkable—though it has to be added that string quartet players, ever on the alert for an imagined loss of pitch, have been known to *plink-plonk* at their strings, even saw away furtively with their bows at the open violin notes of G, D, A and E, in preparation for that loveliest of all movements . . . in D flat. One of Britain's most internationally acclaimed quartets habitually retunes between movements.

As to lesser works, though—a suite by Grieg or a jaunty little serenade by Mozart—one has a strong suspicion that if the composer were to return to earth and experience the deafening silences between movements he would be both puzzled and disappointed. What on earth is gained by preserving a stiff silence between *Anitra's Dance* and *In the Hall of the Mountain King*? And why not give the orchestra a hand after a dashing performance of *Sabre Dance* in Khachaturian's *Gayaneh Suite*?

To return to the Brahms symphony, I suppose in this instance the composer did not want us to break into applause after that majestic opening movement, since he was at pains to end it on a quiet note. There is also a sense in which, given some almost inconclusive ending, we can carry its message more readily through towards the finale, where part of the same material returns, if only in spirit.

As for the two middle movements, they are little more than interludes between the great formal structures of the outer movements. Whoever it was that called architecture 'frozen music', and therefore by implication music 'architecture in motion', might almost have been thinking of this symphony, though he was writing before its composition.

I might add that I am not alone in suggesting that those middle movements are relatively unimportant. Brahms himself cut them down in length during rehearsal so as to throw the outer movements into greater relief.

After the genial second movement and the graceful third, then comes the moment for work to restart on the musical cathedral. We are given a stern hint of the symphony's very opening bars; then a hushed, expectant, tense section sets up the scaffolding on which will be built That Tune, the incomparable theme that begins

Incomparable? On second thoughts I take back the word, because 'comparable' it most certainly is, for all its magnificence. When the devoted Clara Schumann was shown the score in first draft and the composer confessed to her that he was stuck, she pressed him to continue.

'It is full of wonderful beauty,' she said. 'You *must* go on with it.'

'I can't,' Brahms told her, 'with Beethoven marching behind.'

He finished it eventually, of course. But Beethoven certainly was marching behind. The critics were gleeful. 'That big tune in the last movement is taken from a Beethoven symphony!' they cried.

And Brahms retorted, 'Any ass can hear that.'

There *is* a decided similarity between the middle strain of Brahms' great C major tune and part of the finale of Beethoven's ninth. But although similarity between tunes may matter desperately in Tin Pan Alley it is of little consequence in Valhalla. And Valhalla is where we are with Brahms One and Beethoven Nine.

The listener's only regret (or this listener's, at any rate) is that the exigencies of structural form preclude that splendid tune being heard just one more time at the end, in full force, grandly stated, instead of being merely referred to in germinal form. There is just before this a discursive C major passage, as if Brahms were actually toying with the idea of . . . But no. This is the land of the German symphony, not of the *Warsaw Concerto*. We have already heard that fine theme for the last time and must be content.

When the Prom performance ended I trust that then you and your escort applauded both composition and orchestra to the echo, being careful of course to avoid clapping over the final chord as Prom audiences so love to do! Somewhere in every Prom audience, Pat, there is this man—I've no idea who he is—whose mission in life is to prove that he knows which is the last chord of every orchestral item in the repertoire. I imagine him, palms at the ready, waiting to lead his troops into action at a split-second's cue. I would love to meet him one day and shake him by the hand. Believe me, he'd never be able to clap again.

Who did take you to the Prom? (The question sounds like a bad line from an American college movie!) Was it Bix? If so, did he enjoy the *Siegfried Idyll* which I notice opened the second half of the concert? I wonder if he found it a little lacking in impulsion, given his jazz background?

On the other hand, he'd like the richness of the harmonies. My guess is that he enjoyed it, but found it a bit too long. Let's face it—it is.

Your affectionate

Steve

18

My Dear Pat

A great musician once observed that while Wagner undoubt-edly had his heavenly moments he also had his precious dull half hours. And somebody else, after an evening spent in the company of *Parsifal*, or perhaps at one of the *Ring* operas, noted that as a member of a Wagner audience you go into the theatre at six o'clock. Two hours later when you glance at your watch it's twenty past six.

Your word 'enchanting' is just right for the *Siegfried Idyll*. The charming story behind its composition is no doubt part of the magic, though I do think the piece tends rather to go on and on. I even wonder whether Cosima Wagner felt a touch of *ennui* as she lay there in bed listening to the first performance.

It is a delightful story. On Christmas morning 1870, a date which also happened to be his wife's birthday, Wagner gathered a small orchestra on the staircase outside her room and played as a surprise for her and for their one-year-old son Siegfried the musical message of love and gratitude which he had secretly composed in their joint honour. ('For him, and you, I give thanks in Music.')

The small group of musicians playing on the stairs included the great conductor Hans Richter on trumpet, and it so happened that a house guest staying at the Villa Triebschen at

102

the time was the philosopher, Nietzsche. He, in his room, must surely have wondered what was going on, perhaps even quietly cursed his host for organizing a rehearsal so early on Christmas morning.

I have sometimes wondered whether Mrs Wagner was *quite* as surprised by it all as we like to imagine. There are not many mothers of an infant son who can sleep soundly while a bunch of German musicians assemble on a staircase with their instruments, band parts and necessary music stands.

'Keep quiet, Siegfried,' I think she told her son. 'When your daddy has finished hissing at his musicians and kicking the music stands over, he will have a lovely surprise for us.'

Just my imagination perhaps. But now the musicologists, ever ready to spoil a good story, are suggesting that Wagner and his colleagues did not play on the stairs at all but in the *hall* of the villa that memorable Christmas morning. Only one thing we can be sure about: breakfast was late and cook was furious.

The musical experts can be very hard on one's favourite musical stories. I gather that the legend of Debussy putting together the material for *La Mer* while on a visit to Eastbourne, of all places, is now viewed with suspicion. The pianist, Alkan, did *not* after all perish through pulling an enormous bookcase down on himself. Lully did not leave his conductor's podium and crawl on all fours through the ranks of his orchestra in order to bite a recalcitrant double-bass player on the leg.

Any moment now they will be casting doubts on my favourite Wagner story, which tells how the great man was introduced to an extremely minor American composer bearing the unforgettable name of Silas Gamaliel Pratt. According to an eye-witness Wagner shook hands with the worthy Mr Pratt and remarked affably, 'They tell me you are the Richard Wagner of the United States.' To which the American gentleman replied gallantly, 'And you, sir, are the Silas G. Pratt of Germany.' What could have been more courteous? I'm sure they were firm friends from then on.

Not all composers have entertained friendly feelings towards one another, to put it mildly. Their comments on each other make interesting reading; and taken in conjunction, confusing too. Here are a few samples:

Tchaikovsky   I do not regard Bach as a great genius.

Mozart   I learnt to sing from Bach. (But it was J. C. Bach that he meant, not Johann Sebastian.)

Wagner (on J. S. Bach)   The most stupendous miracle in all music.

Tchaikovsky   Handel is only fourth rate, he is not even interesting.

Schumann   Music owes as much to Bach as does religion to its founder.

Berlioz   Bach is Bach, as God is God.

Tchaikovsky   Mozart is the Christ of music.

Chopin (his last words)   Play Mozart in memory of me.

Saint-Saëns   Bach and Mozart—supreme and all-sufficient.

Schubert   O Mozart, immortal Mozart!

Tchaikovsky   I like some things of Haydn.

Haydn (to Mozart's father)   I tell you before God and upon my word as an honest man, your son is the greatest composer I have ever heard of.

Haydn (of Handel)   He is the master of us all!

Mozart (of Beethoven)   Keep your eye on him. He'll make the world talk some day.

Beethoven (to a companion, while listening to Mozart's last piano concerto)   My friend, *we* shall never be able to do anything like that.

Weber   Beethoven is a monster, with no respect for the

nature of instruments. Clarity and precision are meaning-less to him.

Beethoven (hard pressed) I like trees better than people.

Berlioz (on Beethoven's Violin Concerto) Unparalleled beauty.

Chopin Beethoven embraced the universe with the power of his spirit.

Beethoven (on himself) Yes, Beethoven can write music, thank God. But he can do nothing else on earth.

Tchaikovsky I sympathize with Gluck in spite of his poor creative gift.

Bizet Chopin—strange, unique, inimitable.

Bizet again Auber, who had so much talent and so few ideas, was nearly always understood, while Berlioz, who had genius without any talent, hardly ever found under-standing.

Berlioz Wagner is obviously mad.

Rimsky-Korsakov What terrible damage Wagner did by interspersing his pages of genius with harmonic and modulatory outrages!

Ravel I would rather have composed Chabrier's *Le Roi Malgré Lui* than *The Ring of the Niebelung*.

Wagner (on meeting Schumann) It is impossible to discuss anything with a man who will hardly open his mouth.

Schumann (on meeting Wagner) I cannot endure a man who talks incessantly.

Hans von Bulow I believe in Bach the Father, Be 1oven the Son, and Brahms the Holy Ghost of music.

Tchaikovsky This self-inflated mediocrity Brahms! Why, compared to him, Raff is a giant.

Brahms   I should be happy to use as a main theme ideas that Dvorak uses only in passing.

Tchaikovsky   Recently I heard Delibes' masterly *Sylvia*. My *Swan Lake* is small stuff in comparison.

Ravel   If Saint-Saëns had been making shell cases during the war it might have been better for music.

Richard Strauss (on Delius)   I would never have dreamt that anyone but myself could write such good music.

The composers whom most composers seemed able to agree about were Bach, Mozart and Beethoven. When, at a performance of Beethoven's Fifth Symphony, someone exclaimed to Berlioz, 'It is unbelievable . . . Wonderful! Such music should not be written!', the wise Berlioz replied quietly, 'Calm yourself. It will not happen too often.'

And when Mendelssohn played part of the same score to Goëthe on the piano, the poet cried, 'This is tremendous . . . Insane. One would expect the house to fall down!'

Some of the great composers were certainly difficult, dislikeable men. But then, carrying such a load of artistic responsibility as theirs, they were entitled to be. Genius confers privileges.

'I met him the other night in the Café Riche,' wrote someone in the year 1903. 'His face is flat, the top of his head is flat, the eyes prominent, the expression veiled, the beard unkempt, the clothing uncouth.' So much for the composer of *Clair de Lune* and one of the world's greatest string quartets. Proof yet again, should we need it, that the old music hall song spoke the plain truth: you can't tell the marmalade from the label on the jar.

Some musicians were notorious for their prickliness. There is a story about two nineteenth-century composers, Anton Rubinstein and Henryk Wieniawski, who toured as recitalists giving chamber music concerts around the world. They were affable colleagues, indeed great friends, until one day they arrived to play at some American concert hall and saw the posters that had been printed to advertise their visit. On the

106

posters someone had printed Rubinstein's name *very slightly larger* than Wieniawski's name. As a result they fell out, and from that time onwards they never spoke. It was said that they played the *Kreutzer Sonata* together more than seventy times subsequently without once exchanging a word, on or off the platform. So much for the international language of great music!

Composers can be boorish as well as jealous, their manners completely belying the grace or charm of their music. When Dame Sybil Thorndike's brother, Russell, was a boy chorister at Windsor Castle towards the end of the nineteenth century, he was horrified one day to see Sir Arthur Sullivan stride into St. George's Chapel puffing at a large cigar, at the very moment when Queen Victoria was being pushed in at the opposite entrance in her wheelchair. Young Thorndike, only a lad, left his choir stall, snatched the cigar from Sullivan's hand and hissed, 'Silly, I know sir, but it's not really allowed in the nave, you know.'

According to the story, Sullivan never forgot him, and I'm not surprised. I'm only surprised that he didn't stub out his cigar on the lad's surplice. Nevertheless, a majestic royal rebuke was averted.

A handful of gentle, self-effacing composers seem to have been universally loved. Dvorak, who adored trains and time-tables and wrote down engine numbers even when he was over 60; who felt ill at ease among the Latin-sprouting notables when he was given a Doctorate of Music at Cambridge, but then suggested in a letter that '. . . perhaps it is better after all to compose my *Stabat Mater* than to know Latin . . .'; the same mild-mannered Dvorak saw an announcement in the papers that would have reduced most of his colleagues to fury.

It said that the Hellmesberger Quartet were to play a work which he had not yet written. Dvorak's comment?—'I must hurry up and write it.'

The boyishly human Swiss composer, Honegger, while on a visit to London, donned stoker's overalls at King's Cross station and got permission to drive on the footplate of an engine bound for Hitchin in Hertfordshire. For a man whose

Paris flat was covered with pictures of railway engines it must have been a memorable trip.

All these anecdotes, good and bad, merely add up to one hardly surprising conclusion: namely that the clichés about people in general apply equally to the great composers. People *are* funny; it *does* take all sorts to make a world; there *is* good and bad in all of us; you *can't* tell the marmalade. And as Oscar Wilde so pertinently put it, 'The fact of a man being a poisoner is nothing against his prose.'

The gossip and stories about great artists are permissible, I think, because they can sometimes be illuminating, and because in the end they are unimportant and tend in any case to cancel each other out.

That's my excuse, anyway. Even a scurrilous clerihew may occasionally be allowed. For instance:

> *The composer Auber*
> *Was normally sober,*
> *Unlike the painter Watteau*
> *Who was frequently blotteau.*
> *The good Auber spurned the bottle,*
> *Saying 'No thanks—I'm teetottle.'*
>
> *O fortunate Auber!*
> *Unhappy Watteau!*
>
> *Or perhaps notteau.*

One of my very favourite stories about a creative person is about a painter, not a composer. A few days before his death at the fine old age of 87 the painter, Ingres, was found at his drawing-board, despite great weakness, making a pencil copy of a portrait by Holbein.

'Whatever are you doing?' asked someone in consternation.

The old man looked up. 'I am learning,' he replied.

Your affectionate

Steve

19

My Dear Pat

A good deal of our recent correspondence seems to have been about composers and the writing of music rather than about performers and the playing or singing of it. As you say, the former could hardly exist without the latter. People involved in writing *about* music—present company included—tend sometimes to get bogged down with the way scores are notated, rather than the way in which they can best be brought to life. Executants who play and sing music are at least as important as those who create it, and some of us need reminding of the fact from time to time.

Take the unaccompanied Cello Suites of J. S. Bach. They are an intellectual marvel. A musician could read them to himself for ever, like an art lover gazing at a Rembrandt or a saintly person studying his Bible.

But Bach did not write them in order that they should be the academic musician's favourite bedtime reading. One might almost say that he wrote them down on paper because he didn't have a cassette recorder handy. In other words the written score is merely a convenient medium that will bridge the gap between the creative brain of a Bach and the executant fingers of a Pablo Casals.

When Casals first encountered the pieces he was a young

boy thumbing through a pile of miscellaneous scores in a music shop. Suddenly he came across the Cello Suites and opened the first page.

'All I could do was stare at the music,' he said much later. 'Then I took the pieces home. I practised them every day for twelve years. But I was 25 years old before I had the courage to play them in public.'

Solid practice for a dozen years, and only then a public performance! How that shames the rest of us, who often plunge into public performance, whether solo, in instrumental groups or choirs, with the bare minimum of rehearsal and virtually no spiritual or mental preparation. You might even say that we don't *deserve* great music.

When Casals decided that he dared at last to offer the public his interpretations of Bach's unaccompanied cello works, his private pursuit of their riches did not end there. To the end of his days—and that was three-quarters of a century later—he would get up in the morning, open his Bach folios, and try yet again to fathom their mysteries. According to his own statement he never did exhaust them. The chances are that no one ever will.

Famous concert recitalists are not monks (as Artur Rubinstein has abundantly proved in his autobiography). But the detail of the study and preparation required of them is enough to amaze the average concertgoer, who likes to think of them rattling off scales and technical exercises for hours on end but who knows nothing of the silent hours confronting artistic and technical problems.

One has only to take the opening of something like Liszt's *Liebestraum No. 3.* Most of us have played it at one time or another, dwelling lovingly on that juicy tune, doing our brisk best with the knottier cadenzas that intersperse its various appearances.

The tune begins

—but let's hold it there. Notated for the piano, it looks like this—

Two bars of music. But the performance problems fairly crowd in on one another.

First task: find out what the written instructions mean. How is one to approach the piece?

Poco allegro means 'a little on the lively side'. That is a shock right from the start, because one's instinct on approaching anything called *Love's Dream* is to wallow in its sentimentality. But Liszt has forestalled us there. How about *con affetto?* That means 'with affection'. And down in the tenor range where the melody begins, the words *dolce cantando* mean 'sweetly singing'.

So our instructions have begun. Our performance must be lively, yet affectionate and song-like. Not an easy combination to achieve. But there are the composer's plain orders. His orders on how loudly one should begin are much less plain, in fact there is nothing to guide us except the two 'hairpins' which between them tell us to swell the volume over the first bar and drop it over the second. So how loud should the first note be?

That decision is crucial because the whole of the performance hinges on the degree of volume we choose to set for that first note of the melody.

The feeling of weight and tone which the pianist imparts to that preparatory note will have to be intensified for the second note because it must hold clearly through three beats, singing through the five-quaver arpeggio above it. But the moment one has struck a note on the piano it begins to die away. Long notes suffer more 'decay' than short ones. So, however much one may try to achieve

111

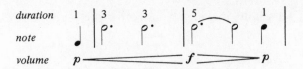

what one is bound to get is more like this—

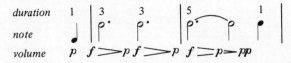

The only way to get a smooth transition from the end of any 'decayed' note to the start of the next is to pick up the tone at the point to which it has died away. Otherwise there will be a bump in the melody line. And who wants that in *Love's Dream*?

The greatest problem of all lies in bar two, where the melody note has to last for a full five beats instead of for three, as its predecessors did. What to do? Thump it out and hope for the best?

No. Give it an extra degree of tone, then move the rest of the bar along at a minutely faster tempo to give impulsion. After all, we know there is a yearning note coming in the third bar which will compensate the listener for losses in this.

But what's this in the left hand? A short note at the start of each bar? Surely that can't be right? Yet it is what's written. And there at the foot of the music is the word *Ped.*, indicating that the note which the composer insists on writing short will ring through the whole bar anyway. Mysterious indeed. Why didn't he write a *full-length* bass note?

The music that I have just described in such detail takes something like five seconds to play; the whole work might take four and a half minutes. Obviously the decisions that the thoughtful player requires to make are enough to occupy his study time for many hours, never mind dashing through scales and arpeggios or breaking off to call his agent for an advance.

These decision processes, believe me, are gone through by recitalists whenever they take a new item into their repertoire. Although the composer's written instructions are invaluable,

112

they can sometimes be a positive hindrance, as on the celebrated occasion where Beethoven writes a piano chord which, like it or not, will immediately start to die away, and then under it adds the word *cresc.*, which means exactly the opposite, namely that the sound is actually to *increase*!

cresc.

What *is* the poor pianist to do? Obviously *think a crescendo*. There is nothing else he can do. In his anxiety to convey a musical feeling, Beethoven has notated a music howler. No great harm in that: theory may be the loser, but art has gained a point at the expense of sign language.

It is not only pianists who have to undergo these tests of decision-making. The singer has additional worries that scarcely even occur to the piano player. The singer is concerned in the expression of words as well as music. He has an accompanist to assist him (but equally to inhibit him on occasions). He must worry about intonation, vocal tone and pitch. Pianists never play out of tune, they merely have to play sometimes on out-of-tune instruments. The singer is his own instrument, and a cold in the head which merely inconveniences a pianist can incapacitate a vocal performer.

This is the moment to break off and enquire whether you have done any singing lately, Pat? When your engagement to that choir conductor came to an end you were understandably annoyed at the way you had been let down. You resigned your membership of the choir. Have you joined another?

I hope so. Like the wings of the penguin, a voice can atrophy if it isn't constantly exercised.

Your affectionate

Steve

20

My Dear Pat

To judge from your most recent letter I had no cause to worry about you neglecting your singing. 'A friend is giving me very interesting lessons from time to time,' you write cryptically. I'm delighted to hear it.

As for your uncle, he's a sport—deciding in middle age that he wants to extend his musical appreciation. I'll certainly help if I can.

It was Sir Thomas Beecham who made the celebrated remark that 'the English may not like music, but they absolutely love the noise it makes'. Quite right too: 'the noise it makes' is what determines our instant appreciation of any given piece of music.

You say your uncle adores the music of Handel, but grows faintly uneasy in the presence of anything much more recent, perhaps one might say more romantic. Given that he would like to enjoy a wider range of music, what is he to do?

The answer is, of course, to move by easy stages. From Handel to Beethoven via Haydn and Mozart is an obvious progression and not a very difficult one to negotiate. From Beethoven's idiom in the *Missa Solemnis* he might try *Elijah*, the Fauré *Requiem*, then Elgar's *Dream of Gerontius*. *Belshazzar's Feast* may seem to him a bit daunting, but many people who can't take that seem able to enjoy *Carmina Burana*. And get him to take a tip from me: get a recording out of the library of the *Requiem* by Maurice Duruflé. I think he'll like it.

A parallel journey in purely orchestral terms might take him from Beethoven's *Pastoral Symphony* through the *St. Anthony Variations* of Brahms to Samuel Barber's *Adagio for Strings*, with the slow movement of Walton's First Symphony as an immediate goal.

But there is a still more rewarding route if your uncle should be alive to the sound of the string quartet, in which repertoire lie the innermost secrets of musical joy. Let him try the bridge from Haydn through Mendelssohn, Debussy and Ravel, to Schoenberg's exquisite *Verklaerte Nacht* in the string sextet version. Extend yourself, uncle . . . Remember Browning!

Walton . . . Schoenberg . . . And beyond?

I have been thinking again about Carl Birdcage and *Monodic Lesions IX*. (That man seems to haunt me!) Was I hard on him? Or did I mislead you into wasting your time in trying to understand music which has nothing to convey to you?

It is a fact that most of us stop suddenly where tonal music gives place to atonal. It's no good serial composers (as they are called) pretending that their music is accessible to the masses; it simply is not, and it probably never will be, since their music is a deliberate rejection of the rules that have governed music for many hundreds of years; indeed they are rules which could be said to be implicit in the very science and mathematics of sound. That they defy those rules is their own responsibility, and quite a heavy one.

Not that they suffer so very grievously. As Michael Church put it so trenchantly in a review in *The Times*:

> Good dinners from the BBC, good dinners from the Arts Council, good dinners from a host of lesser benevolent institutions have seen to it that the *avant-garde* art in Britain and America has remained the province of snobbish little enclaves who cheerfully admit that their public will always be a minute one.

'First the theorizings, then the thing itself,' added Michael Church, of a new and defiantly incomprehensible work. And he ended his review:

> But wide-eyed talk about communication on many levels can never obliterate the fact that at the common denominator level, where the ear is charmed by rhythm and melody, they [the *avant-garde* composers] scarcely communicate at all.

How true. What is music *for*, anyway?

It is there to please, to delight, to refresh, to entertain. I once remember hearing the principal of the Royal Academy of Music addressing a school speech day on the subject of music and its appreciation. 'Music,' he announced baldly, 'is for fun—it has no other justification.' Consternation among the members of staff—I thought the headmistress was about to have hysterics. Music for fun? No other justification? Was the man mad?

He was not. He was making an excellent point, though in a manner calculated to catch the wandering attention of three hundred schoolgirls in a hot marquee.

Music *is* for fun . . . or for enjoyment, if you feel the need to substitute a grander word than fun. Enjoyment can come equally from a Josquin motet, a Sousa march, an Oscar Peterson blues or a Queen single, depending on the state of your ears and your arteries. Even, I admit it, from Birdcage and his *Lesions*. Mr Birdcage, too, has his followers, and a highly effective pressure group they seem to be.

Music is a big, broad, beautiful, many-splendoured thing, Pat. After all my arguments and qualifications through our correspondence to date I hope we haven't ever lost sight of the fact that music is—in Sydney Smith's delicious expression—'The only cheap and unpunished rapture on earth.'

As you leave for your (surely rather hastily arranged?) holiday to wherever-it-is, I must admit that I shall miss you and your letters. I had no idea you were contemplating going

116

away. Will you be alone, or with a friend? If the latter, I hope
he or she is a friend to music as well as to you.

Bon voyage, my dear Pat. Can you spare me just one more
letter before you go, telling me all about it?

Ever your affectionate

Steve

To MR AND MRS CARL BIRDCAGE
ORCHID ROOM CONFERENCE SUITE
CARLTON CENTRE HOTEL LONDON W1

WARMEST CONGRATULATIONS AND GOOD WISHES ON YOUR MARRIAGE.

MUSIC LOVERS WILL BE LOOKING FORWARD TO EPITHALAMIUM I.

HAVE A GOOD TRIP.   STEVE RACE